SMP **11-16**

Book Y5
new edition

CAMBRIDGE
UNIVERSITY PRESS

Published by the Press Syndicate of the University of Cambridge
The Pitt Building, Trumpington Street, Cambridge CB2 1RP
40 West 20th Street, New York, NY 10011–4211, USA
10 Stamford Road, Oakleigh, Melbourne 3166, Australia

© Cambridge University Press 1987, 1993

First published 1987
Third printing 1990
New edition 1993
Reprinted 1994

Printed in Great Britain at the University Press, Cambridge

A catalogue record of this book is available from the British Library

Illustrations by Dick Bonson, Chris Evans and David Parkins
Photographs by John Ling and Paul Scruton
Cover photograph by Tick Ahearn
Diagrams and phototypesetting by Parkway Group, London
and Abingdon, and Gecko Limited, Bicester

ISBN 0 521 45741 6 paperback

Contents

1 Surfaces

A Developable surfaces: the cylinder

Roughly speaking, a **developable** surface is one we can make out of a piece of paper, without stretching the paper at all.

For example, the label on a soup tin starts as a rectangle. It is printed while it is still flat. Then it is wrapped round the tin and becomes a cylinder. So the curved surface of a cylinder is a developable surface.

In the process the paper is curved but the design and the letters are not distorted. Three things stay the same or, as we say, are **preserved**.

1 **Distances** in any direction are preserved.

   In fact, the circumference of the cylinder is just the length of the rectangle (assuming no overlap), and the height of the cylinder is the height of the rectangle.

2 **Angles** are preserved.

   For example, the two angles shown here are right-angles on the flat rectangle, and they still remain right-angles on the cylinder.

3 **Areas** are preserved.

   The coloured area is exactly the same on the cylinder as it is on the flat rectangle.

   In fact, the curved surface of the whole cylinder is the same area as the rectangle, again assuming no overlap.

Suppose a tin can has a diameter of 72 mm.
A rectangle which just wraps round it with no overlap must have a length equal to the circumference of the tin, that is $\pi \times 72\,\text{mm} = 226\,\text{mm}$ (to the nearest mm).

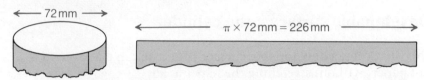

A1 Calculate the length of a rectangle which will just wrap round a cylindrical tin of diameter 80 mm.

A2 A rectangle of length 60 mm is rolled into a cylinder. Calculate the diameter of the cylinder.

The helix

Draw a straight line on a rectangular piece of paper. Roll the rectangle into a cylinder.

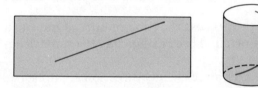

The line becomes part of a curve called a **helix**.

The helix can be seen in many places, for example

a bolt,  a twisted strip of paper.

It is also the path of a tip of a ship's propeller as the ship moves along at a steady speed.

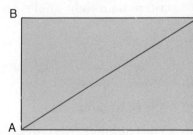

A3 The diagram on the left shows a line which is drawn round a cylinder. This line is called a helix. The point B is directly above A.

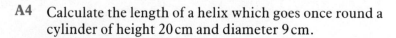

If the cylinder is cut along AB and flattened into a rectangle, the helix becomes a diagonal of the rectangle.

(a) Calculate the length of the diagonal of the rectangle.

(b) Draw the rectangle with its diagonal full size. Cut it out. Make it into a cylinder.

A4 Calculate the length of a helix which goes once round a cylinder of height 20 cm and diameter 9 cm.

A helix crosses every circle parallel to the base of the cylinder at the same angle.

We can find this angle by trigonometry. The next question shows how.

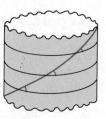

A5 A helix goes once round a cylinder of height 4 cm and diameter 3 cm.

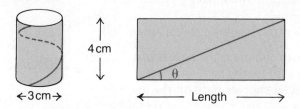

Calculate the angle marked θ.

A6 A helix goes once round a cylinder of diameter 8·5 cm and height 10·2 cm. Calculate the angle that the helix makes with the base.

A7 A helix goes once round a cylinder of **radius** 10 cm. If the helix makes an angle of 30° with the base, how high is the cylinder?

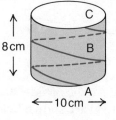

A8 Suppose a helix goes twice round a cylinder of diameter 10 cm and height 8 cm, as shown on the left.
If the cylinder is cut along ABC and flattened, we get a rectangle which looks like this.

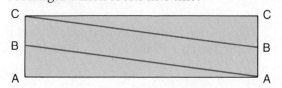

(a) Calculate the length of the helix.

(b) Calculate the angle it makes with the base.

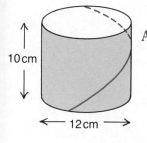

A9 The diagram on the left shows a helix which goes only halfway round a cylinder of diameter 12 cm and height 10 cm.

Draw the flattened-out cylinder and calculate the length of the helix and the angle it makes with the base.

A10 If this helical spring is straightened out, how long will the wire be?

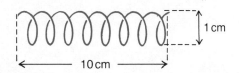

3

B Shortest paths

A spider and a fly are crawling about on a gutter.
The gutter is half of a cylinder, of diameter 12 cm
and length 100 cm.

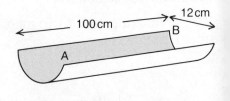

The spider is at A and the fly at B. What is the
shortest path on the gutter from A to B?

To find out, we imagine the gutter unrolled into
a rectangle.
The shortest path must be along the diagonal AB.

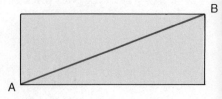

On the actual gutter the diagonal becomes a
helix, but it must still be the shortest path.
If there were an even shorter path on the gutter
this would correspond to a path on the rectangle
shorter than the diagonal, because all distances
are preserved when the gutter is unrolled. But
there can be no shorter path than the diagonal.

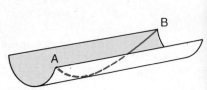

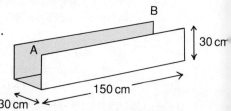

B1 This time the spider and fly are on
the square-section gutter shown here.

Find the length of the shortest path
on the gutter from A to B.

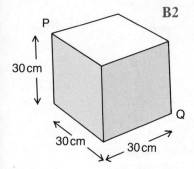

B2 Now they are at opposite corners P, Q of a cube of side 30 cm.
Two possible paths on the cube from P to Q are shown below.

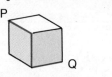

Find the length of the shortest path.
How many shortest paths are there?

4

B3 The diagrams below show a cuboid 5 cm by 6 cm by 3 cm, and a net for it.

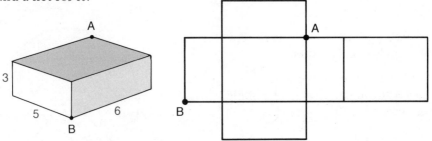

(a) Draw the net (a sketch will do) and mark the point A as shown. There are **three** points on the net corresponding to B on the cuboid. Mark each of them with a B.

(b) What is the shortest distance from B to A on the surface of the cuboid?

B4 A and B are on opposite sides of a long cylinder of diameter 30 cm.

A is 10 cm from one end of the cylinder and B is 20 cm from the end.

Calculate the length of the shortest path on the cylinder from A to B.

(Imagine the cylinder is cut and flattened out.)

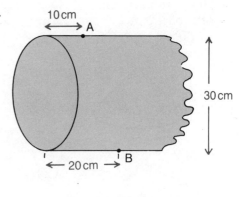

B5

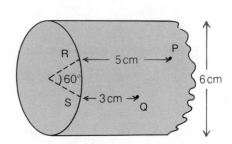

*B6 Repeat question B4, but this time the cylinder is an open-ended cardboard tube with A on the outside but B on the **inside**.

C Developable surfaces: the cone

Draw a circle of radius 4 cm.

Draw two lines from the centre, at right-angles to each other.

Cut out the shape shown here. It is a **sector** of the circle. The angle of the sector is 270°.

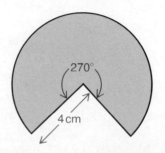

By placing the two straight edges together, make the sector into a **cone**.

The radius of the sector, 4 cm, becomes the **slant height** of the cone.

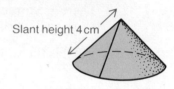

The base of the cone is a circle.

The circumference of the base . . .   . . . is equal to the length of the **arc** of the sector . . .   . . . which is ¾ of the circumference of the circle with radius 4 cm.

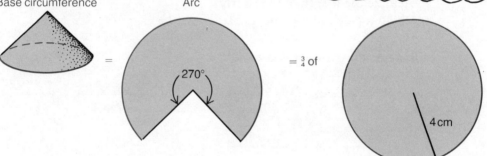

Base circumference   Arc

$= \frac{3}{4}$ of

4 cm

C1 (a) Calculate the circumference of the circle with radius 4 cm.

(b) Calculate the length of the arc of the 270° sector of this circle.

(c) The answer to (b) is the base circumference of the cone. Divide it by 2π to find the base radius of the cone.

You should find that the base radius of the cone is ¾ of the radius of the sector (¾ of 4 cm).

If you think about it, this is the result you would expect. The base circumference is ¾ of the larger circle's circumference, so the base radius will be ¾ of the larger circle's radius.

(The circumference of a circle is directly proportional to its radius.)

We get a similar result when the sector has a different angle.

This sector is ⅓ of a circle of radius 6 cm.

When the sector is made into a cone the base radius will be ⅓ of 6 cm, or 2 cm.

This is because the base circumference has to be ⅓ of the circumference of the 6 cm circle.

C2 If this semi-circle is made into a cone, what will the base radius of the cone be?

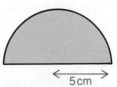

C3 (a) What fraction of a complete circle is this sector?

(b) If the sector is made into a cone, what will the base radius of the cone be?

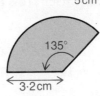

We can use the same idea 'in reverse' to calculate the angle of the sector given the slant height and base radius of the cone.

In this cone the base radius is $\frac{6}{10}$ of the slant height.

So the cone is made from $\frac{6}{10}$ of a circle of radius 10 cm.

The angle of the sector is $\frac{6}{10}$ of 360° = **216°**.

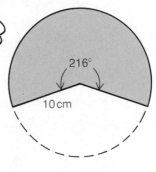

C4 Calculate the angle of the sector needed to make a cone with

(a) base radius 4 cm and slant height 5 cm

(b) base radius 10 cm and slant height 18 cm

(c) base radius 0·4 cm and slant height 2 cm

7

Shortest paths on a cone

A termite has found its way blocked by a conical ant-hill. The termite is at A and needs to crawl to the diametrically opposite point B. What is the shortest possible path?

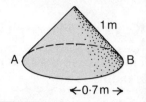

1 m

A   B

← 0·7 m →

| A path round the base has length $\frac{1}{2} \times 2\pi \times 0·7$ m, or about 2·2 m. 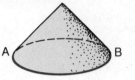 | A path over the top has a length of 2 m. 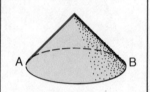 | But the shortest path goes across the curved surface of the cone. 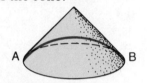 |

Imagine the cone is made of paper. If it is cut through A and flattened out, we get a sector.

The shortest path from A to B on the sector is also the shortest path on the cone, because distances are preserved when the cone is flattened out. On the cone itself, this path is a curve.

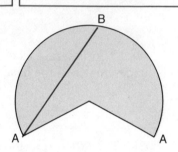

C5 (a) Calculate the angle of the sector above.

(b) Calculate the length of AB to the nearest 0·1 m.

C6 Find the shortest distance on this cone

(a) from A to B   (b) from A to C

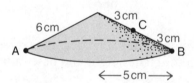

6 cm   3 cm   C

3 cm

A   B

← 5 cm →

2 Optimisation

A 'Bin-packing' problems

A1 There are 200 people at a conference who are to go on a coach trip.
Each coach has 50 passenger seats.
It is a very simple matter to work out that 4 coaches are needed.

Now suppose we change the problem by adding some restrictions.
The 200 people come from the following countries:

29 French	26 German	31 American	27 Canadian
20 Italian	18 Japanese	24 British	25 Dutch

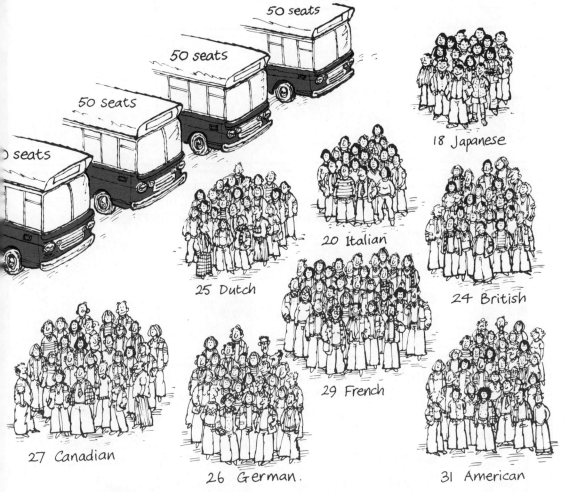

People of the same nationality must all sit together.
More than one nationality may share a coach.

Work out how many coaches are needed now.

The coach problem is an optimisation problem. ('Optimisation' means finding the best possible way of doing something.)

Coaches are expensive to hire, so the 'best' solution to the problem is one which uses the smallest number of coaches.

You may have found the problem very easy to solve, but similar problems can be much more difficult.
Here is a way to think of the problem, and other problems like it.

Think of the coaches as 'bins', each 50 units high.

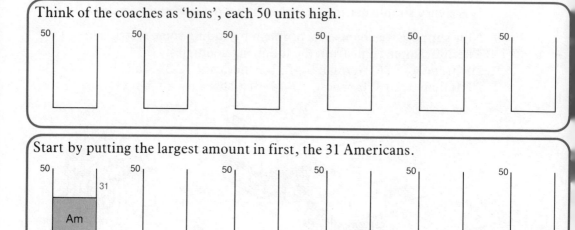

Start by putting the largest amount in first, the 31 Americans.

The largest amount is more than half the capacity of the bin.
Any other amount which is more than half the capacity of a bin will need a new bin. So we need a new bin for the 29 French, for the 27 Canadians and for the 26 Germans.

Now we have some choice as to what to do next. But we cannot get all the other four amounts into the four bins we have used so far. We must use a fifth bin.

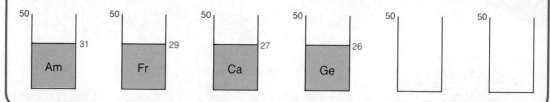

Here is one possible solution.

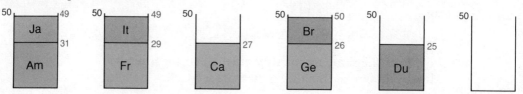

10

There are many other problems which can be thought of as 'bin-packing' problems.

In a 'bin-packing' problem there is often a huge number of ways of packing the items into the 'bins'. But it is not always obvious, when you have an answer, whether it is the best possible packing, that is, the one which uses the smallest number of bins.

Bin-packing problems occur in industry and commerce, where people are always looking for ways to minimise costs. Real-life packing problems often have so many items to be packed that the only way to solve the problem is to use a computer. The questions in this section involve small numbers of items. They are designed to give you a flavour of this type of problem.

The first step is to decide what the 'bins' are – it is not always clear. For example, think about this problem:

  A carpenter has a supply of planks, each 200 cm long.
  He needs to cut out pieces of the following lengths:
   145 cm 95 cm   92 cm   89 cm   71 cm
   109 cm 73 cm   132 cm   58 cm   56 cm

What is the minimum number of planks he can use?

We can think of each plank as a 'bin' 200 units high.
The ten given lengths are the items which have to be 'packed' into the bins.

A2 (a) Solve the problem to find the minimum number of planks.

  (b) How much wood is wasted?

A3 A firm's delivery van can carry up to 2 tonnes.
The following loads have to be carried to a customer:

Load	A	B	C	D	E	F	G	H	I	J
Weight in tonnes	1·7	1·2	0·8	1·5	0·4	0·7	0·1	1·8	0·3	1·5

  (a) What is the smallest number of journeys which will be needed to deliver all the loads?

  (b) The firm would like the last journey to be as lightly loaded as possible, to leave room for some other items. Show how this can be done.

A4 A plumber wishes to cut twelve pieces of copper pipe. They are to be cut from standard 3-metre lengths.

Piece	A	B	C	D	E	F	G	H	I	J	K	L
Length in metres	$\frac{1}{2}$	$\frac{1}{2}$	$\frac{3}{4}$	$\frac{3}{4}$	$\frac{3}{4}$	$\frac{3}{4}$	1	1	1	$1\frac{1}{2}$	$1\frac{3}{4}$	$1\frac{3}{4}$

  (a) What can you think of as the 'bins' in this problem?

  (b) What is the smallest number of 3-metre lengths the plumber can use? Show how the pieces would be cut.

11

A5 A TV company plans its programmes so that breaks for adverts are no longer than **2 minutes**. They have to fit in the following adverts, whose lengths are given in seconds.

Cereal	50	Cars	36	Margarine	35	Chocolate	25
Cream	50	Bread	36	Detergent	35	Newspaper	24
Sausages	50	Holidays	36	Hair spray	35	Bacon	24
Paint	50	Crisps	36	New film	32		
Tyres	36	Video	36	Tissues	32		

(a) What is the minimum number of advertising breaks needed? Show how you would make up each break (e.g. 50, 25, 24).

(b) How long is the longest advert which could be added to the list without increasing the number of breaks?

Bin-packing problems can be solved using a computer to go through all the possible ways of packing the items and to find the best way. But when the number of items is very large, the process can take a lot of computer time and be very expensive.

In practice it may not be worth trying to find the **best** solution to a problem: a good solution may be enough, if it saves computer time. The method usually used for bin-packing problems is called the 'decreasing first fit' method. It does not necessarily yield the best possible solution (the one which uses fewest bins), but it does lead to a solution which uses only up to 20% more bins than the minimum.

The basis of the method can be set out as a flowchart loop:

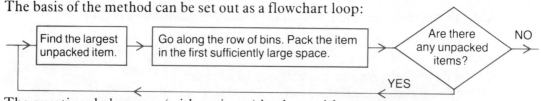

The questions below may (with patience) be done without a computer. But if you have access to a computer and are able to program it, then use it.

A6 Items of information are to be 'packed' in computer storage units. Each item of information consists of a number of characters. Each storage unit can hold up to 300 characters.

The numbers of characters in each item of information are as follows:

175	205	24	138	45.	62	18	241	215	111	106
51	24	62	189	105	77	29	43	99	162	205
9	125	176	49	58	33	149	153	122	56	92

Ideally, the number of storage units used should be as small as possible. Use the 'decreasing first fit' method to pack the items into units.

A7 Another bin-packing method is called the 'decreasing best fit' method. Instead of packing the largest unpacked item into the first large enough space, we pack it into the fullest bin it will fit into. Use this method to do question A6.

B Maximisation subject to a constraint

B1 A woman is escaping from a foreign country. She has a knapsack and can carry only a limited weight (4·0 kg).

She has a number of items which she would like to carry away with her. They have different weights and different values.

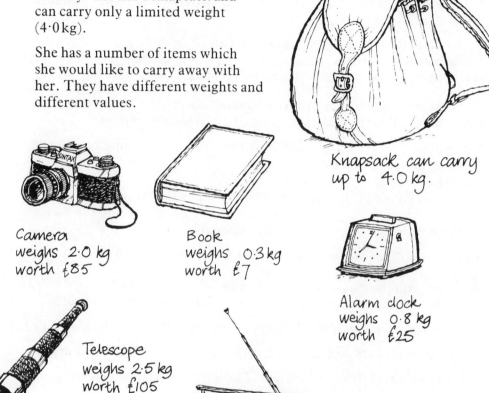

Knapsack can carry up to 4·0 kg.

Camera weighs 2·0 kg worth £85

Book weighs 0·3 kg worth £7

Alarm clock weighs 0·8 kg worth £25

Telescope weighs 2·5 kg worth £105

Radio weighs 1·6 kg worth £47

(a) What items should she pack to make the load as valuable as possible?

(b) What will her load be worth?

B2 Suppose the woman has several of each item instead of just one of each. The items have the same weights and values as before.

Now she has to decide, for example, **how many** telescopes to take, not whether to take a single telescope or not. She also has to do this for the other items.

(a) What should she now pack to make the load in the knapsack as valuable as possible?

(b) What will the load be worth?

In questions B1 and B2 you were asked to maximise the value of the load while at the same time making sure that the weight did not exceed 4 kg.

We say that you were trying to maximise the value, subject to the **constraint** that the weight should not exceed 4 kg. ('Constraint' is another word for 'restriction'.)

Problems of the type given in question B2 are often difficult, because you may not be sure that you have found the best possible combination of items. Perhaps there is a combination which you haven't thought of which is even better.

The only way to be sure is to have a method of going through all the possibilities. A method like this is called a **systematic** method.

We shall first describe a systematic method for solving a simpler problem, in which there are only two kinds of item.

Jim has £3 to spend on chocolate.

He has a choice of two types: Radbury's 70 g bars, costing 45p each,
Cowntree's 130 g bars, costing 80p each.

He wants to get as much chocolate as possible.

The constraint here is that the total cost must not exceed £3.

1 Start with the maximum possible number of one of the bars.
(The working is shorter if you start with the more expensive bar.)

The maximum number of Cowntree bars is **3**, because 4 would cost £3·20.

3 Cowntree bars cost £2·40, leaving enough money for **1** Radbury bar.

The weight of this combination (3 Cowntree, 1 Radbury) is **460 g**.

2 Now reduce the number of Cowntree bars by one, and find the maximum number of Radbury bars which can be bought as well.

2 Cowntree bars cost £1·60, leaving enough money for **3** Radbury bars.

The weight of this combination (2 Cowntree, 3 Radbury) is **470 g**.

3 Now reduce the number of Cowntree bars by one again. As before, find the maximum number of Radbury bars which can be bought as well. Continue until the number of Cowntree bars is 0, and the maximum possible number of Radbury bars is bought.
The results can be set out in a table.

Number of Cowntrees	Number of Radburys	Weight
3	1	460 g
2	3	470 g

and so on

B3   (a) Copy this table and complete it.
      (b) What is the greatest weight, and which combination gives it?

14

B4 A van costs £55 to hire and will carry up to 1·5 tonnes.
A lorry costs £90 to hire and will carry up to 2·5 tonnes.

Find the maximum weight which can be carried if the total
hire cost must not exceed £400.

The method used so far can be extended to problems where there are three
kinds of item to choose from. Here is an example.

A carpenter can make three
kinds of item. This table shows
the time it takes to make each
one, and the amount of profit
he makes.

Item	Time taken	Profit
Garden seat	$1\frac{1}{2}$ days	£15
Dining table	3 days	£60
Stool	2 days	£35

If he has a maximum of 10 days in which to work, what should he
make to maximise his profit?

The constraint here is a time constraint: he has a maximum of 10 days.
The most time-consuming item is the dining table. So start with the
maximum possible number of those. (This shortens the working.)

Dining tables	Stools	Garden seats	Profit
3	0	0	£180
2	2	0	£190
	1	1	£170
	0	2	£150
1			

The maximum number of tables is 3, leaving no time for anything else.

Reduce the number of tables by one. Maximise the number of stools.

Then reduce the number of stools by one.

And then by one again.

Now reduce the number of tables by one again, and continue as before.

B5 Complete the solution of the problem.

B6 A firm exports three kinds of machine.
Their weights and the costs of exporting them are shown in this table.

	Pneumatic drill	Grinder	Chainsaw
Weight	26 kg	12 kg	8 kg
Export cost	£72	£30	£10

A second firm is exporting an empty boiler. They offer to pack it
with machines up to a weight limit of 100 kg, and carry them free.
What should be packed, to save as much as possible in export costs?

15

3 Algebraic fractions

A Sums and differences of fractions

You will be familiar with the process of 'multiplying out' an expression such as $3(a+b)$.

$$3(a+b) = 3a + 3b$$

The same kind of process can also be applied to expressions such as $\dfrac{a+b}{4}$,

because $\dfrac{a+b}{4}$ can be thought of as $\frac{1}{4}(a+b)$.

$$\frac{a+b}{4} = \tfrac{1}{4}(a+b) = \tfrac{1}{4}a + \tfrac{1}{4}b$$

But $\frac{1}{4}a + \frac{1}{4}b$ can also be written as $\dfrac{a}{4} + \dfrac{b}{4}$, so we get

$$\frac{a+b}{4} = \frac{a}{4} + \frac{b}{4}$$

This is just common sense really, as you can see if you replace a and b by numbers. For example, if you divide 40 + 8 by 4, the result is the same as if you divide 40 by 4 and 8 by 4 and add the two answers.

There is nothing special about 4. The denominator can be any number.

$$\frac{a+b}{c} = \frac{a}{c} + \frac{b}{c}$$

Sometimes we can do some simplifying after we have 'split' a fraction in this way. For example

$$\frac{2a+3b}{ab} = \frac{2a}{ab} + \frac{3b}{ab} = \frac{2a}{ab} + \frac{3b}{ab} = \frac{2}{b} + \frac{3}{a}$$

What we have done here is to re-write, or **express**, the single algebraic fraction $\dfrac{2a+3b}{ab}$ as the sum of two simpler fractions.

A1 Express $\dfrac{3x+6y}{xy}$ as the sum of two fractions and simplify each of the two fractions.

A2 Express each of these as the sum or difference of two fractions, and simplify where possible.

    (a) $\dfrac{ab+ac}{bc}$ (b) $\dfrac{3p-6q}{3pq}$ (c) $\dfrac{p^2+q^2}{pq}$ (d) $\dfrac{3x+1}{x}$ (e) $\dfrac{6a-4}{2a}$

It is sometimes useful to be able to reverse this process, and replace the sum of two algebraic fractions by a single fraction.

If the denominators of the two fractions are equal, there is no difficulty.

For example, $\dfrac{a}{p} + \dfrac{2b}{p} = \dfrac{a+2b}{p}$.

But if the denominators are different, as for example in $\dfrac{2}{b} + \dfrac{3}{a}$, things are not quite so simple.

Look back at the worked example on the opposite page (above question A1).

In that example, we started with $\dfrac{2a+3b}{ab}$ and expressed it as $\dfrac{2}{b} + \dfrac{3}{a}$.

If we want to go backwards, we have to put in a step which makes the two denominators equal, like this:

$$\dfrac{2}{b} + \dfrac{3}{a}$$

Multiply top and bottom by a.   Multiply top and bottom by b.   So that now both of the denominators are equal.

$$= \dfrac{2a}{ab} + \dfrac{3b}{ab}$$

$$= \dfrac{2a+3b}{ab}.$$

Compare this with adding two 'arithmetical' fractions, such as $\frac{2}{5} + \frac{1}{3}$.

$$\dfrac{2}{5} + \dfrac{1}{3}$$

Multiply top and bottom by 3.   Multiply top and bottom by 5.

$$= \dfrac{6}{15} + \dfrac{5}{15}$$

$$= \dfrac{6+5}{15} = \dfrac{11}{15}$$

A3 Write each of these expressions as a single algebraic fraction.

(a) $\dfrac{1}{x} + \dfrac{1}{y}$ (b) $\dfrac{1}{2} + \dfrac{1}{a}$ (c) $\dfrac{a}{b} - \dfrac{1}{c}$ (d) $\dfrac{x}{y} + \dfrac{u}{v}$ (e) $\dfrac{1}{3} - \dfrac{s}{t}$

(f) $2 + \dfrac{1}{x}$ (g) $\dfrac{1}{2a} + \dfrac{3}{b}$ (h) $\dfrac{3}{x} - 1$ (i) $\dfrac{x}{2} + \dfrac{2}{x}$ (j) $\dfrac{u}{v} - \dfrac{v}{u}$

A4 The formula $\dfrac{1}{f} = \dfrac{1}{u} + \dfrac{1}{v}$ is used in physics.

(a) Express $\dfrac{1}{u} + \dfrac{1}{v}$ as a single fraction.

(b) Re-write the formula in the form $f = \ldots$

Worked example

Express $\dfrac{x}{6} + \dfrac{4}{3y}$ as a single fraction.

We will make both denominators $6y$, because both 6 and $3y$ divide exactly into $6y$.

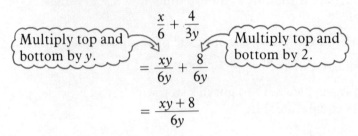

$$\dfrac{x}{6} + \dfrac{4}{3y}$$

Multiply top and bottom by y.   Multiply top and bottom by 2.

$$= \dfrac{xy}{6y} + \dfrac{8}{6y}$$

$$= \dfrac{xy + 8}{6y}$$

A5   Express $\dfrac{a}{2b} + \dfrac{c}{8}$ as a single fraction.

A6   Express each of these as a single fraction.

(a) $\dfrac{x}{3} - \dfrac{y}{12}$ (b) $\dfrac{a}{3x} + \dfrac{b}{xy}$ (c) $\dfrac{5}{a} + \dfrac{2}{ab}$ (d) $\dfrac{1}{p} - \dfrac{3}{p^2}$

A7   Express each of these as a single fraction.

(a) $\dfrac{3}{2a} + \dfrac{5}{a^2}$ (b) $\dfrac{x}{3a} + \dfrac{y}{2ab}$ (c) $\dfrac{y}{4x} - \dfrac{1}{2xy}$ (d) $\dfrac{a}{3x^2} - \dfrac{1}{xy}$

A8   The formula $\dfrac{1}{R} = \dfrac{1}{R_1} + \dfrac{1}{R_2}$ is used in electricity calculations.

(a)   If R_1 is $0\cdot2$ and R_2 is $0\cdot4$, calculate the value of $\dfrac{1}{R}$, and from this the value of R.

(b)   Express $\dfrac{1}{R_1} + \dfrac{1}{R_2}$ as a single fraction involving R_1 and R_2.

(c)   Re-write the formula in the form $R = \ldots$

(d)   Use your re-written formula to calculate R when R_1 is $0\cdot2$ and R_2 is $0\cdot4$, and check that the answer agrees with your answer to part (a).

A9 u, v and f are connected by the formula $\dfrac{1}{u} + \dfrac{1}{v} = \dfrac{1}{f}$.

u, v and m are connected by the formula $v = mu$.

Show that $\dfrac{1}{f} = \dfrac{m+1}{mu}$, and write a formula for u in terms of f and m.

Worked example

Express $\dfrac{3}{x+1} + \dfrac{4}{x+2}$ as a single fraction.

We make both denominators $(x+1)(x+2)$.

Multiply top and bottom by $x+2$.

$$\dfrac{3}{x+1} \quad + \quad \dfrac{4}{x+2}$$

Multiply top and bottom by $x+1$.

$$= \dfrac{3(x+2)}{(x+1)(x+2)} + \dfrac{4(x+1)}{(x+1)(x+2)}$$

$$= \dfrac{3(x+2)+4(x+1)}{(x+1)(x+2)} = \dfrac{3x+6+4x+4}{(x+1)(x+2)} = \dfrac{7x+10}{(x+1)(x+2)}$$

A10 Express $\dfrac{3}{x} + \dfrac{2}{x+1}$ as a single fraction.

A11 Express each of these as a single fraction.

(a) $\dfrac{2}{a} + \dfrac{1}{b+1}$ (b) $\dfrac{3}{x} + \dfrac{1}{x+y}$ (c) $\dfrac{x}{a} - \dfrac{x}{a+2}$

(d) $\dfrac{x}{3} + \dfrac{2}{x-1}$ (e) $\dfrac{2}{x+2} + \dfrac{3}{x-1}$ (f) $\dfrac{5}{x-3} - \dfrac{2}{x+1}$

*A12 A mathematician invents a new notation for writing reciprocals.
She uses $\overline{a}$ to mean $\dfrac{1}{a}$.

So, for example, $a\overline{b}$ means $a \times \dfrac{1}{b}$ or $\dfrac{a}{b}$;

$(a+b)\overline{c+d}$ means $(a+b) \times \dfrac{1}{c+d}$ or $\dfrac{a+b}{c+d}$.

(a) Write these in ordinary notation.

    (i) $ab\overline{c}$ (ii) $a\overline{bc}$ (iii) $(p+q)\overline{r}$ (iv) $p + q\overline{r}$ (v) $\overline{p+\overline{q}}$

One advantage of this new notation is that fractions can be printed on one line only.

(b) Write these in the new notation, using one line only for each one.

    (i) $\dfrac{1}{xy}$ (ii) $\dfrac{x}{y+z}$ (iii) $\dfrac{x}{z} + y$ (iv) $\dfrac{a}{b} + \dfrac{c}{d}$ (v) $\dfrac{a+b}{c}$.

(c) Which of these equations are true for **all** values of a, b and c?

    (i) $\overline{ab} = \overline{a}\overline{b}$ (ii) $\overline{a+b} = \overline{a} + \overline{b}$ (iii) $(a+b)\overline{c} = a\overline{c} + b\overline{c}$

    (iv) $a(\overline{b+c}) = a\overline{b} + a\overline{c}$ (v) $a\,\overline{b+c} = a\overline{b} + a\overline{c}$ (iv) $\overline{\overline{a}} = a$

19

B Equations involving algebraic fractions

Worked example

Solve the equations (a) $\dfrac{x+8}{5} = x$ (b) $\dfrac{x+3}{5} = \dfrac{x}{4}$

(a) To get rid of the '÷5' on the left-hand side, we multiply both sides by 5.

$$\text{So} \quad x + 8 = 5x$$
$$8 = 4x$$
$$2 = x$$

(b) We can get rid of the '÷5' on the left and the '÷4' on the right by multiplying both sides by 20.

$$\frac{20(x+3)}{5} = \frac{20x}{4}$$

$$4\ \frac{20(x+3)}{5} = 5\ \frac{20x}{4}$$

$$4(x+3) = 5x$$
$$4x + 12 = 5x$$
$$12 = x$$

B1 Solve each of these equations.

(a) $\dfrac{x}{2} = x - 3$ (b) $\dfrac{x+1}{3} = x$ (c) $\dfrac{x-4}{5} = x$

B2 Solve each of these equations.

(a) $\dfrac{x+2}{3} = \dfrac{x}{2}$ (b) $\dfrac{x-3}{5} = \dfrac{x}{2}$ (c) $\dfrac{x-2}{5} = \dfrac{x+1}{2}$

Worked example

Solve the equation $\dfrac{2}{x} = \dfrac{3}{x-5}$.

First method	**Second method**
Multiply both sides by x and by $x - 5$. In other words, multiply both sides by $x(x-5)$. $$\frac{2x(x-5)}{x} = \frac{3x(x-5)}{x-5}$$ $$2(x-5) = 3x$$ and so on.	Take the reciprocal of both sides. $$\frac{x}{2} = \frac{x-5}{3}$$ Now multiply both sides by 6, and so on.

B3 Solve each of these equations.

(a) $\dfrac{5}{x} = \dfrac{4}{x-2}$ (b) $\dfrac{3}{x+1} = \dfrac{7}{x}$ (c) $\dfrac{8}{x-3} = \dfrac{3}{x+1}$

C Similar triangles

If the angles of one triangle are equal to those of
another, then the two triangles are **similar**.
Each triangle is an enlargement (or reduction) of
the other.

In the diagram on the right, ABC and A′B′C′ are
similar triangles. They have been lettered so that
the angles at A and A′ are equal, and so on.

The sides AB and A′B′ are opposite the equal angles
C and C′. We say that AB and A′B′ are
corresponding sides of the two triangles.

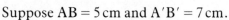

Suppose AB = 5 cm and A′B′ = 7 cm.
We can calculate the scale factor of the enlargement from ABC to A′B′C′
by working out $\frac{7}{5} = 1\cdot4$.

In other words, the scale factor is the ratio $\dfrac{A'B'}{AB}$.

We could also work out the scale factor using $\dfrac{B'C'}{BC}$ or $\dfrac{A'C'}{AC}$.

The three methods must give the same scale factor, so

$$\frac{A'B'}{AB} = \frac{B'C'}{BC} = \frac{A'C'}{AC}.$$

In problems involving similar triangles, it helps to use the letters A, B, C
and A′, B′, C′ to letter the triangles, so that the equal angles get the same
letter (either dashed or undashed).

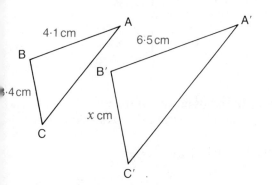

C1 If we apply the equation $\dfrac{A'B'}{AB} = \dfrac{B'C'}{BC}$
to the diagram on the left, we get

$$\frac{6\cdot5}{4\cdot1} = \frac{x}{3\cdot4}.$$

Multiply both sides by 3·4 to get
$$\frac{6\cdot5 \times 3\cdot4}{4\cdot1} = x.$$

Calculate x, to 1 d.p.

C2 Suppose in the diagram above that BC = 2·6 cm, AC = 4·7 cm,
B′C′ = 3·2 cm and A′C′ = x cm.

Calculate the value of x, to 1 d.p.

Worked example

Calculate the length marked x in this diagram.

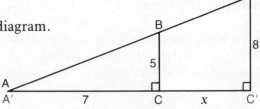

Two similar triangles have been picked out and lettered ABC and A'B'C'. (A and A' are the same point.) We use $\dfrac{A'C'}{AC} = \dfrac{B'C'}{BC}$.

$$A'C' \text{ is } 7 + x, \text{ so } \quad \frac{7+x}{7} = \frac{8}{5}$$

$$\frac{7+x}{7} = 1.6$$

Multiply both sides by 7. $7 + x = 11.2$

$$x = 4.2$$

C3 Calculate a in the diagram on the right.

C4 Calculate x in the diagram below.

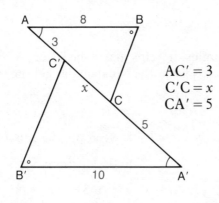

$AC' = 3$
$C'C = x$
$CA' = 5$

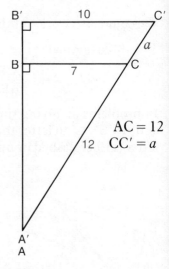

$AC = 12$
$CC' = a$

C5 (a) In the diagram on the left, which other triangle is similar to triangle DAC?

(b) Explain why $\dfrac{h}{p} = \dfrac{y}{x+y}$.

(c) Use another pair of similar triangles to write down an expression for $\dfrac{h}{q}$ in terms of x and y.

(d) Explain why $h\left(\dfrac{1}{p} + \dfrac{1}{q}\right) = 1$.

(e) Calculate h when $p = 4$ and $q = 5$.

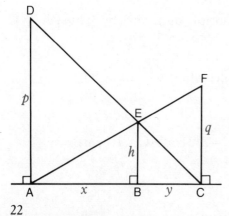

22

C6 The shaded part of this diagram is a rectangle 4 units by 5 units.

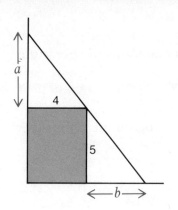

(a) Write down another ratio in the diagram which is equal to $\frac{a}{5}$.

(b) Explain why $ab = 20$.

C7 Use similar triangles to get an equation connecting x and y in this diagram.

Re-write the equation so that it contains no fractions or brackets.

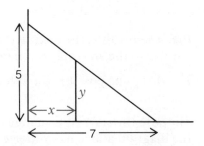

C8

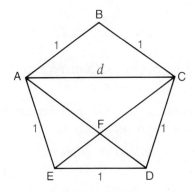

ABCDE is a regular pentagon, whose sides are each 1 unit long.

Each diagonal is of length d units.

In a regular pentagon, each diagonal is parallel to one of the sides of the pentagon.

(a) What kind of shape is ABCF, and what is the length of CF?

(b) Explain why the length of EF is $d - 1$.

(c) Which triangle is similar to triangle EFD?

(d) Use the pair of similar triangles to write an equation for d, and show that the equation can be re-written as $d^2 - d - 1 = 0$.

(e) Measure the diagram to find a rough value for d. (Remember that each side is 1 unit long, and d has to be measured in the same units.)

Use trial and improvement to find d, correct to 2 decimal places.

Two special kinds of rectangle

C9 The 'A-series' of paper sizes has an interesting feature.

If you take a sheet of one of the sizes, say A4, . . . fold it in half, . . . and turn it round,

then the result is the next size in the series (A5) and it is **similar** to the starting rectangle.

For this to be possible the sides of the rectangle have to be in a certain ratio.

Suppose the starting rectangle in the diagram above has a shorter side 1 unit long and a longer side p units long.

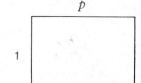

(a) Write down the shorter and longer sides of the 'half-rectangle' after it has been turned round as shown above.

(b) From the fact that the starting rectangle and the 'half-rectangle' are similar, write down an equation for p, and solve it.

(c) Measure the sides of an A4 sheet and check that their ratio is correct.

C10 A 'golden' rectangle has this special feature:

If you cut a square from it, . . . the rectangle which is left is similar to the original rectangle.

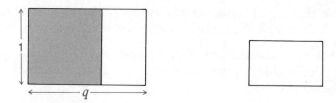

Suppose the original rectangle is 1 unit by q units.

(a) Write down the sides of the rectangle left after the square has been removed.

(b) Write down an equation for q and solve it by trial and improvement.

Back of an envelope 1

1   Here are some calculations Isha scribbled on the back
    of an envelope. Try to figure out what is happening.

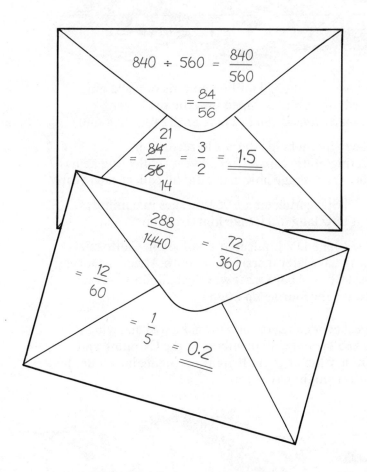

$$840 \div 560 = \frac{840}{560}$$

$$= \frac{84}{56}$$

$$= \frac{\overset{21}{\cancel{84}}}{\underset{14}{\cancel{56}}} = \frac{3}{2} = \underline{\underline{1{\cdot}5}}$$

$$\frac{288}{1440} = \frac{72}{360}$$

$$= \frac{12}{60}$$

$$= \frac{1}{5} = \underline{\underline{0{\cdot}2}}$$

Use a method like Isha's to help you find the answers to
these without using a calculator.

(a) $\dfrac{1620}{648}$ (b) $\dfrac{126}{168}$ (c) $1680 \div 480$

Check your answers with a calculator.

2   Try these. Check your answers by multiplying.

(a) $144 \div 360$ (b) $3240 \div 144$ (c) $128 \div 512$

Solve these problems,
but **don't** use a calculator – just pencil and paper!

3 (a)

Every year about 350 million pounds of packaging
and fishing gear is dumped into the sea.
How many tons is this? (There are 2240 lb in a ton.)

(b) Helge Friholm holds the world record for
collecting bottle caps. After 34 years collecting he has
34 306. On average how many did he collect each year?

(c) In 1974 Steve Meltzer ate 96 sausages in 6 minutes.
About how long did it take him to eat one?

(d) In 1972 Jane Dorst released a balloon in California.
Twenty days later it arrived in South Africa, a journey
of 14 500 km. About what was the balloon's average
speed for the journey in km/h?

4 The longest ever conga or human snake was one which
involved 8659 people, all members of the Camping and
Caravanning Club of Great Britain. Estimate how long this
human snake might have been.

5 The world's largest collection of can ring pulls is 710 000!
Their owner laid them all out in a straight line.
About how many miles long do you think the line was?
(There are 5280 feet in a mile.)

4 Saving and borrowing

A Saving

When you pay money into a bank 'deposit account' (or a building society) it earns interest. The bank pays you for being able to use your money. The bank lends the money to other people or businesses, who pay the bank even more interest than the bank pays you, and in that way the bank covers its costs and makes a profit.

You may wonder why you can't lend your money directly to the other people or businesses, and get the higher interest rate yourself. You can do, but it is usually a more risky affair. If the business goes bankrupt, you lose your money. Banks lend to many different companies and can afford to take the occasional risk.

Banks and building societies have various savings schemes, each with its **annual interest rate**.

Suppose you invest £500 in a building society, and the interest rate is 8% p.a. (p.a. = per annum, or per year).

After 1 year the amount invested is multiplied by **1·08**.
So after 1 year the amount is £500 × 1·08 = £540.

After 1 more year, the amount is multiplied by 1·08 again,
so after 2 years it is £540 × 1·08 = £583·20, and so on.

> **A1** Dawn invests £80 in a bank deposit account. The interest rate is 6% p.a. Calculate the amount in Dawn's account after 3 years, to the nearest penny.

Jim invests £5000 in a bank. The interest rate is 8% p.a.
If Jim leaves the money in the bank for 1 year, the amount would be £5000 × 1·08 = £5400.

Jim decides to leave his £5000 in the bank for six months only.
You might think the bank should pay half the yearly rate of interest, that is 4% for six months. Suppose the bank does this.

After six month's Jim's amount is £5000 × 1·04 = £5200.

After another six months, his amount is £5200 × 1·04 = **£5408**.

Suppose Jim now decides to leave his money in the bank for another six months.

But this is more than Jim would have got by leaving his money in for 1 year at 8% per year!

The reason for the discrepancy is this: an increase of 4% followed by another increase of 4% is **not** equivalent to an increase of 8%.

This is because multiplying by 1·04 and then by 1·04 again is equivalent to multiplying by 1·04 × 1·04, or 1·0816, and this means an increase of **8·16%**, not 8%.

If the yearly interest rate is 8%, the six-monthly rate has to be 3·923%, because

$$1·039\,23 \times 1·039\,23 = 1·08.$$

> This is the **square root** of 1·08.

A2 Calculate the **three-monthly rate**, when the yearly rate is 8%.

B Borrowing

Suppose you want to buy something expensive. You may decide to borrow the money from a bank. The bank will charge you interest on the loan. The higher the rate of interest, the costlier is the loan.

A simple kind of loan is one which is made for a fixed period, and where the borrower repays the full amount, including interest, at the end of the period.

For example, suppose Anar borrows £500 for 4 years, and the interest rate is 20% p.a.

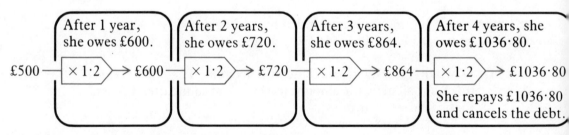

A more common way to repay a loan is by **instalments**.
Suppose John borrows £100. The interest rate is 15% p.a. He agrees to repay £30 at the end of each year until the debt is cancelled.

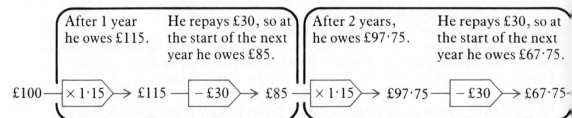

B1 Continue the calculation above and find out how many years it takes John to repay the loan.

28

In the previous question, you were given the interest rate and the size of the instalments and were asked to find out how long it would take to repay the loan.

In practice we start from the interest rate and the time to full repayment, and calculate the size of the instalments.

Worked example

Karl borrows £400. The interest rate is 20% p.a.
He agrees to repay in two equal instalments, one after 1 year and the other after 2 years. Calculate the instalment.

Let each instalment be £I.

After 1 year, Karl owes £400 × 1·2 = £480.
He then repays £I, so at the start of the next year he owes £$(480 - I)$.

After 2 years, Karl owes £$(480 - I) \times 1 \cdot 2$
$$= £(480 \times 1 \cdot 2 - I \times 1 \cdot 2)$$
$$= £(576 - 1 \cdot 2I)$$

He then repays £I and cancels the debt. So

$$576 - 1 \cdot 2I - I = 0$$
$$576 - 2 \cdot 2I = 0$$
$$576 = 2 \cdot 2I$$

$$\frac{576}{2 \cdot 2} = I$$

$$I = 261 \cdot 82 \text{ (to 2 d.p.)}$$

So Karl pays two yearly instalments of **£261·82**.

B2 Rowena borrows £1000. The interest rate is 24%.
She agrees to repay in two equal yearly instalments.
Calculate the instalments.

B3 Sam borrows £1000. The interest rate is 20%. He agrees to repay in three equal yearly instalments of £I.

(a) Show that after 2 years, just before the second instalment is paid, Sam owes £$(1440 - 1 \cdot 2I)$.

(b) Write down an expression for the amount Sam owes just after the second instalment is paid.

(c) Show that after 3 years, just before the third instalment is paid, Sam owes £$(1728 - 2 \cdot 64I)$.

(d) The third instalment cancels the debt. Write an equation which says this and solve it to find the value of I.

Most personal loans are repaid in monthly instalments.
When people buy things on **hire purchase** they are being given a loan by a
hire purchase company. The repayments are usually monthly.

The interest rate for loans is usually called the **annual percentage rate** (APR).
The table below shows the size of monthly instalments when £100 is borrowed
at various different APRs.

Time to full repayment

		1 year	2 years	3 years	4 years	5 years
	20%	£9·19	£5·01	£3·63	£2·96	£2·56
	22%	£9·27	£5·09	£3·72	£3·05	£2·65
APR	24%	£9·35	£5·17	£3·80	£3·13	£2·75
	26%	£9·42	£5·25	£3·89	£3·22	£2·84
	28%	£9·50	£5·33	£3·97	£3·31	£2·93
	30%	£9·58	£5·41	£4·06	£3·40	£3·03

To find the monthly instalments for loans of amounts other than £100,
you scale up or down.
For example, the instalments for a loan of £250 are 2·5 times those for a loan of £100.

B4 What are the monthly instalments for a loan of £850 at
APR 24% repaid over 3 years?

B5 What are the monthly instalments for a loan of £80 at APR 28%
repaid over 2 years?

The table can be used to find (approximately) the annual percentage rate of
interest when you are told the monthly instalments and the repayment period.

B6 A company offers a loan of £500, to be repaid in monthly
instalments of £15·30 over a period of 4 years.

(a) What would the monthly instalments be if the loan were
£100 instead of £500?
(b) Use the table above to find the APR, approximately.

B7 The cash price of a car is £3500. If you pay £500 now you
can have a loan to cover the rest of the price. The loan is to
be repaid in 36 monthly instalments of £117. Find the APR.

B8 Which of these loans has the lower APR?
A: a loan of £800 repaid in 24 monthly instalments of £42
B: a loan of £800 repaid in 36 monthly instalments of £30·40

Companies offering loans are legally required to state the APR.
This enables the would-be borrower to compare the costs of loans.

5 Area under a graph

A Step-graph approximations to a curve

Imagine that we have a video screen and we want to 'draw' the curve shown on the right.

We have a pen or 'plotter' which can only move across → and up ↑ .
The distance across each time is 5 mm, but it can be moved up any distance.

So the plotter is able to draw 'step-graphs', like this, for example:

The plotter can draw a 'step-graph approximation' to the curve above in two different ways.

(1) It can start by going 5 mm across, then up to the curve, then across again, and so on.

This produces a step-graph which is everywhere below the curve (except at the points where it touches the curve).

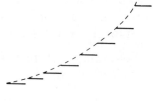

(2) Or it can start by going up, then 5 mm across to the curve, then up again, and so on.

This produces a step-graph which is everywhere above the curve.

The curve itself is 'sandwiched' between the 'lower' and 'upper' step-graphs.

Each of the two step-graphs, the upper and the lower, is a kind of approximation to the curve itself. Step-graphs will become important in the work which follows.

B The area under a graph

An architect has designed an exhibition hall whose roof has the shape of the graph of the function $x \rightarrow 25 - 0{\cdot}02x^2$ between $x = {}^-20$ and $x = 20$.

x is the distance in metres measured sideways from the centre line of the hall.

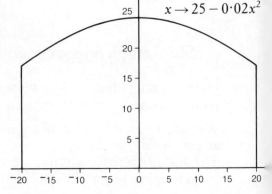

$x \rightarrow 25 - 0{\cdot}02x^2$

In order to design the air-conditioning system, the architect needs to know the volume of the hall. She knows its length (75 m), so she needs to find its **cross-sectional area**.

The cross-sectional area is the area under the graph of $x \rightarrow 25 - 0{\cdot}02x^2$ between $x = {}^-20$ and $x = 20$.

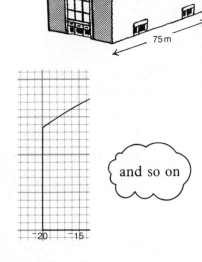

75 m

One way to find this area would be to plot the graph on squared paper, and count the squares under the graph.

For example, if the graph is drawn like this, each small square stands for $1\,\text{m}^2$.

and so on

This method is time-consuming and requires accurate drawing. A method based on calculation would be better.

Here is one method which can be used.
The cross-section of the hall is symmetrical, so we need to find the area of only one half of it.

1 Split the area into vertical strips of equal width. (The width of each strip here is 5 m.)

We can use the formula $x \rightarrow 25 - 0{\cdot}02x^2$ to find the height of each of the vertical lines.

Let f stand for the function $x \rightarrow 25 - 0{\cdot}02x^2$.
Here is a table of values of f(x).

x	0	5	10	15	20
f(x)	25	24·5	23	20·5	17

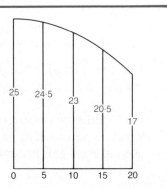

2 Draw the step-graph which starts horizontally and then drops after 5 m across, 10 m across, and so on.

The area under this step-graph can be calculated. It will be larger than the area under the curve itself.

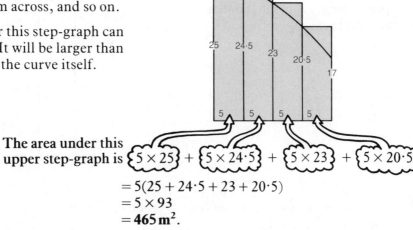

The area under this upper step-graph is $\{5 \times 25\} + \{5 \times 24{\cdot}5\} + \{5 \times 23\} + \{5 \times 20{\cdot}5\}$

$= 5(25 + 24{\cdot}5 + 23 + 20{\cdot}5)$
$= 5 \times 93$
$= \textbf{465 m}^2.$

3 Draw the step-graph which starts by dropping and then going 5 m horizontally.

The area under this lower step-graph is less than the area under the curve itself.

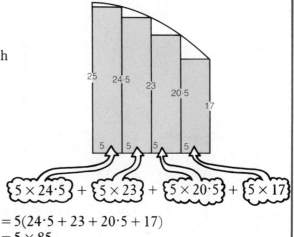

The area under this lower step-graph is $\{5 \times 24{\cdot}5\} + \{5 \times 23\} + \{5 \times 20{\cdot}5\} + \{5 \times 17\}$

$= 5(24{\cdot}5 + 23 + 20{\cdot}5 + 17)$
$= 5 \times 85$
$= \textbf{425 m}^2.$

4 The area under the curve itself is between 425 m² and 465 m². We could take the mean of these two values as a reasonable approximation. So the area is approximately $\dfrac{425 + 465}{2} = \textbf{445 m}^2.$

B1 (a) Calculate the area under the upper step-graph here.
   (b) Calculate the area under the lower step-graph.
   (c) Write down an approximate value for the area under the curve.

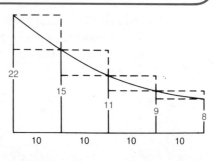

33

B2 Use the method of upper and lower step-graphs to calculate an approximate value for the area under this curve.

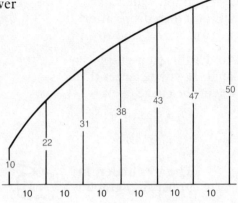

B3 The diagram below shows part of the graph of the function q, where $q(x) = 2 + 0 \cdot 1x^2$.

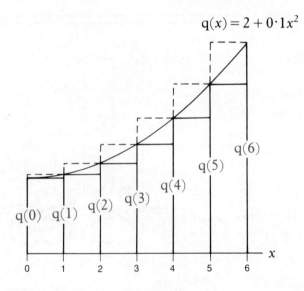

$q(x) = 2 + 0 \cdot 1x^2$

(a) Calculate the values of $q(0)$, $q(1)$, $q(2)$, . . . up to $q(6)$.

(b) Calculate the area under the upper step-graph.

(c) Calculate the area under the lower step-graph.

(d) Find an approximate value for the area under the graph of $q(x)$ between $x = 0$ and $x = 6$.

(e) Do you think your answer to part (d) is slightly greater, or slightly smaller, than the actual area under the graph? How can you tell which it is, from the shape of the graph?

We can get a better approximation to the area under a graph by using narrower strips, so that the step-graphs approximate more closely to the graph itself.

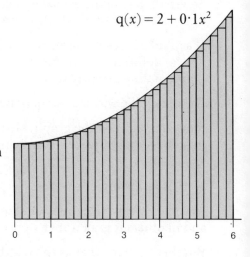

$q(x) = 2 + 0.1x^2$

The diagram on the right shows the same graph as in question B3. The strips are each of width 0·2.

Only the lower step-graph is shown. As the strips are made narrower (so that there are more and more of them), the area under the lower step-graph increases and gets closer and closer to the area under the graph itself.

Similarly the area under the upper step-graph (not shown here) decreases and gets closer and closer to the area under the graph itself.

When there are a large number of very narrow strips, the calculation of the area under the step-graph is very tedious, but simple on a computer or programmable calculator.

This program can be used to print out the area under the **lower** step-graph when W, the width of each strip, is 0·2.

X is used for x, Y for q(x), A for the area of a strip and T for the total area so far.

To print out the area under the **upper** step-graph, replace the second line by
        20   FOR X = W TO 6 STEP W

```
10  LET W = 0·2
20  FOR X = 0 TO 6 – W STEP W
30  LET Y = 2 + 0·1 * X * X
40  LET A = W * Y
50  LET T = T + A
60  NEXT X
70  PRINT T
```

To get a better approximation to the area under the graph itself, reduce the width of a strip.

Here are some results obtained using the BASIC program. A spreadsheet could also have been used.

Width of strip	Area under upper step-graph	Area under lower step-graph
0·2	19·564	18·844
0·1	19·381	19·021
0·01	19·2180098	19·1820098
0·001	19·1962018	19·192603
0·0001	19·2001619	19·1998019

B4 Program a computer or calculator to calculate an approximation to the area under the graph of the function r(x) = $x^3 + 1$, between $x = 0$ and $x = 5$.

35

So far all the graphs we have looked at in this chapter have sloped one way, either upwards throughout or downwards throughout.

If a graph slopes upwards in some parts and downwards in others, we can define a step-graph which approximates to the shape of the graph in the following way:

Decide on the width of strip to be used, say 0·5.

Start at a point on the graph. Go across 0·5, then **either** up **or** down (whichever it has to be) to meet the graph. Then go across 0·5 again and so on.

Here is an example.

In some places this is a lower step-graph and in others it is an upper step-graph.

But it is still true that as the width of the strips is reduced, the area under the step-graph gets closer and closer to the area under the graph itself.

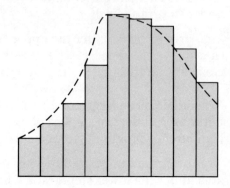

The calculation of the area under the step-graph can be carried out in the following way:

Suppose the graph is the graph of a function f(x).
Suppose x starts at a and ends at b and the width of the strips is w.

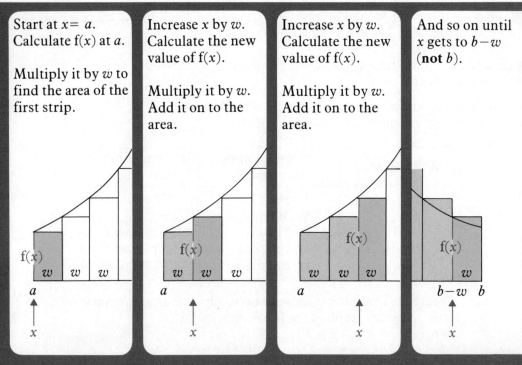

| Start at x= a. Calculate f(x) at a.

Multiply it by w to find the area of the first strip. | Increase x by w. Calculate the new value of f(x).

Multiply it by w. Add it on to the area. | Increase x by w. Calculate the new value of f(x).

Multiply it by w. Add it on to the area. | And so on until x gets to b−w (**not** b). |

B5 This diagram shows the graph of the function $s(x) = x^2(3 - x)$.

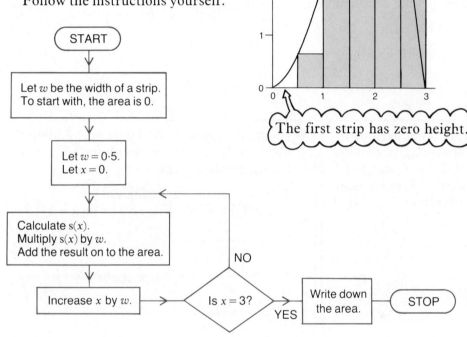

$s(x) = x^2(3 - x)$

It also shows an approximating step-graph, with strips of width $0·5$.

(a) The flowchart below shows how to calculate the area under the step-graph.
Follow the instructions yourself.

START

Let w be the width of a strip. To start with, the area is 0.

Let $w = 0·5$. Let $x = 0$.

Calculate s(x). Multiply s(x) by w. Add the result on to the area.

Increase x by w. → Is $x = 3$? → NO

Write down the area. STOP

YES

The first strip has zero height.

(b) Re-do the calculation with $w = 0·2$.

(It can be shown that the actual value of the area is **6·75**.)

B6 Calculate an approximation to the area under the graph of $y = x(4 - x)$ between $x = 0$ and $x = 4$, using strips of width

(a) $0·5$ (b) $0·2$

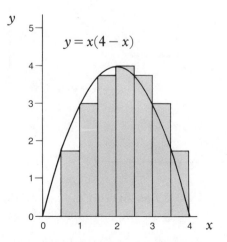

$y = x(4 - x)$

C The trapezium rule

The work in this section involves calculating the areas of **trapeziums**.
A trapezium is a quadrilateral with one pair of parallel sides.

Let a and b be the lengths of the parallel sides
of a trapezium, and let h be the distance
between them (measured at right-angles to them).

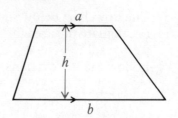

The area of the trapezium is given by the formula

$$\text{Area} = \tfrac{1}{2}h(a + b).$$

There are several different ways of explaining why this formula is correct.
Here is one way.

1 Draw a line across the
trapezium, parallel to
the parallel sides and
halfway between them.
Call its ends P and Q.

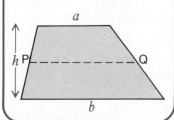

2 Rotate the top section of the trapezium through 180°
about Q. It then joins up with the bottom section to
form a parallelogram.

The base of this parallelogram is $a + b$.
The height is $\tfrac{1}{2}h$. So its area is $\tfrac{1}{2}h(a + b)$.

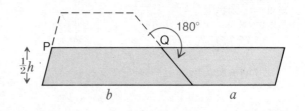

C1 Calculate the area of each of these trapeziums.

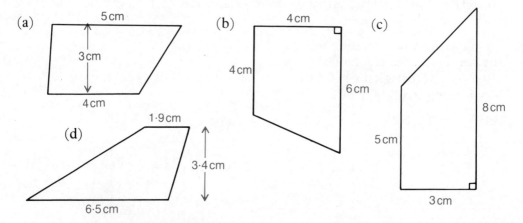

C2 What sort of 'trapezium' do you get when $a = 0$?
Does the formula for the area still work in this case?

The **trapezium rule** is another method of calculating, approximately, the area under a curve. Here is an example to explain the method.

Suppose we want to find the area under the curve shown on the right.

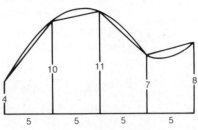

As before, we split the area into strips of equal width. Here the width of each strip is 5.

We replace the curve by a set of straight lines as shown. The area under this set of straight lines is an approximation to the area under the curve.

Each of the four shapes A, B, C and D is a trapezium. So we can use the formula $\frac{1}{2}h(a+b)$ to find the area of each one.

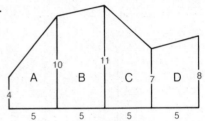

h is 5 for each trapezium.

Area A $= \frac{5}{2}(4+10)$

Area B $= \quad \frac{5}{2}(10+11)$

Area C $= \qquad \frac{5}{2}(11+7)$

Area D $= \qquad\quad \frac{5}{2}(7+8)$

The areas have been set out like this on purpose, so that you can see an 'overlapping' pattern. For example '10' comes into the expression for area A and for area B.

We can set out the complete calculation of the total area like this:

$\frac{5}{2}(4+10$
$\qquad + 10 + 11$
$\qquad\qquad + 11 + 7$
$\qquad\qquad\qquad + 7 + 8)$

The reason why the three 'middle' heights each occur twice in the brackets is because each is a side of two trapeziums, one on the left and one on the right.

The **trapezium rule** for an approximation to the area under a graph is

$$\frac{\text{Width of strip}}{2} \times (\text{1st height} + 2 \times \text{each intermediate height} + \text{last height})$$

The result for the curve above is $\frac{5}{2}(4 + 2 \times 10 + 2 \times 11 + 2 \times 7 + 8) = \mathbf{170}$.

C3 Use the trapezium rule to find an approximation to the area under the curve on the right.

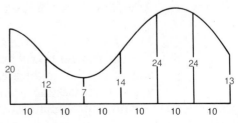

39

C4 A metalworker has designed a scoop.

The curved part of the scoop is made from a piece of sheet metal whose shape is shown in the diagram below, which is $\frac{1}{2}$ **full size**.

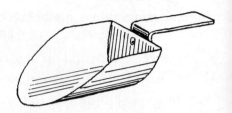

Scale: $\frac{1}{2}$ full size

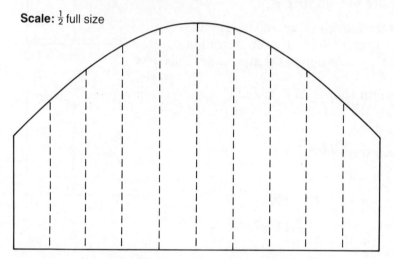

Take measurements from the drawing and calculate an approximation to the area of the piece of metal, using the trapezium rule. Remember that the scale of the drawing is $\frac{1}{2}$ full size.

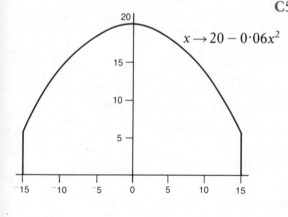

$x \rightarrow 20 - 0{\cdot}06x^2$

C5 The roof of an aircraft hangar has the shape of the graph of $x \rightarrow 20 - 0{\cdot}06x^2$ between $x = {}^{-}15$ and $x = 15$.

(Measurements are in metres.)

(a) Calculate the height of the roof at $x = 0$, $x = 5$, $x = 10$ and $x = 15$.

(b) Use the trapezium rule to find an approximation to the cross-sectional area of the hangar.

(c) The hangar is 150 m long. Calculate its volume, approximately.

C6 (a) At what values of x does the graph of $x \rightarrow (x - 1)(5 - x)$ cross the x-axis?

(b) Sketch the shape of the graph between these two points.

(c) Use the trapezium rule with strips of width $0{\cdot}5$ to calculate an approximation to the area under the graph between the two points where it crosses the x-axis.

(d) Is your approximate value too large or too small? How can you tell?

D Area under a graph of (time, speed)

A car travels at a constant speed of 4 m/s for 6 seconds.

The graph on the right is a (time, speed) graph for the car. It shows that the speed stayed constant at 4 m/s during the 6 seconds.

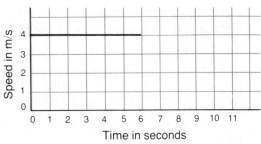

During the 6 seconds the car, going at 4 m/s, travelled a distance of 24 metres.

This distance, 24 m, is represented in the graph by the **area** under the graph, which is the area of a rectangle 4 by 6.

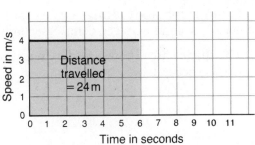

Suppose the car's speed suddenly drops to 2 m/s, and the car goes on at 2 m/s for 4 seconds.

The extra distance, 8 m, is represented by the extra area under the graph.

(Of course, a sudden drop in speed like this is not physically possible.)

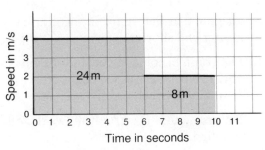

D1 Calculate the distance travelled by each of the cars whose (time, speed) graphs are shown below.

(a)
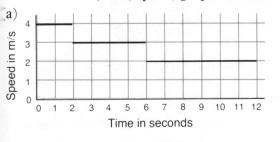

(b)
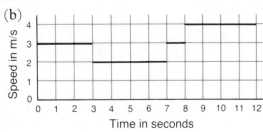

(c)
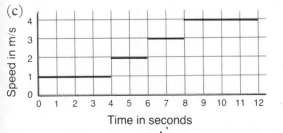

(d)
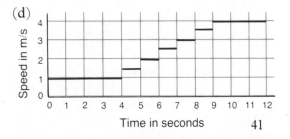

41

The car shown in this graph goes at 1 m/s for 1 second.
Then it goes a little faster for 1 second.
Then it goes a little faster for 1 more second, and so on.

After 8 seconds, its speed has reached 5 m/s.

The shaded area under the graph shows the distance travelled in the 8 seconds.

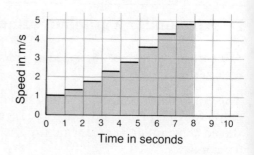

In this graph, the car increases its speed after every $\frac{1}{2}$ second between 0 and 8 seconds.

The shaded area shows the distance it travels in the 8 seconds.

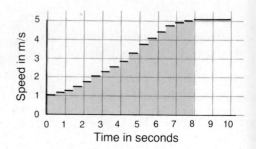

Imagine that the 'steps' in the graph get shorter and shorter.

The graph becomes a continuous curve which shows the car's speed increasing gradually between 0 and 8 seconds.

The area under the graph shows the distance travelled.

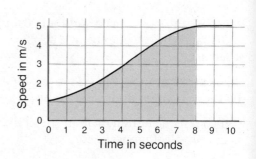

> Distance travelled = Area under (time, speed) graph

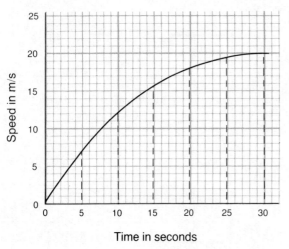

D2 This is the (time, speed) graph of a train leaving a station.

Use the trapezium rule to calculate approximately the distance travelled by the train in 30 seconds.

Use strips of width 5. Notice that the first height is 0.

D3 A train is travelling at 30 m/s when the brakes are applied. t seconds after applying the brakes the speed of the train is $30 - 0 \cdot 3t^2$ m/s. The (time, speed) graph looks like this.

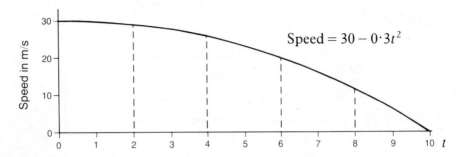

Calculate the speed at 2-second intervals and use the trapezium rule to calculate approximately the distance travelled by the train during braking.

If the vertical axis shows the rate of flow of water in litres per second, and the horizontal axis shows time in seconds, then the area under the graph represents the amount of water in litres which flows in a given period of time.

D4 The rate of flow of water from a hosepipe varied during a period of 60 seconds as shown in the graph below.

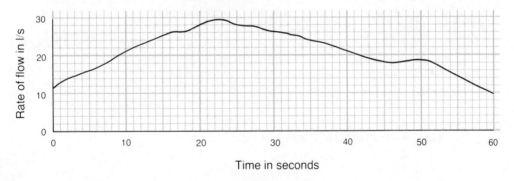

Use the trapezium rule with strips of width 10 to calculate approximately the volume of water which flowed from the hosepipe during the 60 seconds.

D5 The rate of flow of water, r litre/min, from a tank is given by the formula $r = 10 \times 2^{-t}$, where t is the time in minutes from when the tap is opened.

(a) Calculate r when t is 0, 1, 2, 3, 4 and 5.

(b) Use the trapezium rule to estimate the volume of water which flows from the tank in the first five minutes.

Review 1

1 Surfaces

1.1 This diagram shows the curved surface of a cylinder, of radius 5 cm and height 10 cm.

(a) Calculate the area of the curved surface.

(b) The helix goes once round the cylinder. Calculate its length.

(c) Calculate the angle which the helix makes with the base of the cylinder.

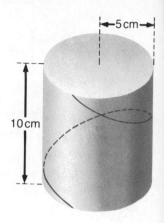

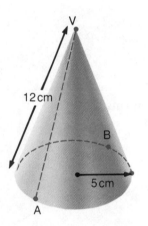

1.2 The cone shown here is cut along the line AV and flattened out.

(a) Sketch the flattened-out shape.

(b) Calculate the angle of the sector.

(c) The point B is diametrically opposite A. Draw the sector to scale and measure the shortest distance on the cone from A to B.

1.3 This diagram shows a cube whose edges are 5 cm long.
The point B is at the centre of a face.

Calculate the shortest distance from A to B on the surface of the cube.

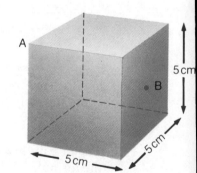

Optimisation

2.1 A plumber has copper pipes in standard lengths of 200 cm.
She needs pieces of these lengths (in cm):

130   110   100   75   75   70   70   65   60   50   45

(a) Her first priority is to use as few standard lengths as possible.
What is the smallest number she will need?

(b) When she cuts the standard lengths up, there will be some waste.
The waste is more useful if it is in a few long pieces than in a
lot of short pieces. So her second priority is to achieve this.
Find the best way of cutting the standard lengths.

2.2 A truck can carry up to 1000 kg.
Cookers weigh 200 kg and are worth £140. Fridges weigh 160 kg and
are worth £120. Washing machines weigh 300 kg and are worth £200.

What is the most valuable load the truck can carry?

Algebraic fractions

3.1 Express each of these as the sum or difference of two fractions,
and simplify the fractions where possible.

(a) $\dfrac{3a + 12b}{4}$ (b) $\dfrac{a^2 + b^2}{ab}$ (c) $\dfrac{3x - 2y}{xy}$ (d) $\dfrac{3a - 2a^2}{a^2}$

3.2 Express each of these as a single fraction.

(a) $\dfrac{2}{x} + \dfrac{3}{y}$ (b) $\dfrac{3}{x} + \dfrac{1}{x^2}$ (c) $\dfrac{3}{ax} - \dfrac{2}{bx}$ (d) $\dfrac{a}{p} + \dfrac{b}{pq}$

(e) $\dfrac{3}{x} + \dfrac{2}{x + 1}$ (f) $\dfrac{4}{x} - \dfrac{3}{x - 1}$ (g) $\dfrac{3}{a} + \dfrac{2}{b + 1}$ (h) $\dfrac{4}{x - 2} - \dfrac{2}{x + 3}$

3.3 Solve each of these equations.

(a) $\dfrac{x}{7 \cdot 3} = \dfrac{4 \cdot 2}{1 \cdot 6}$ (b) $\dfrac{5 \cdot 3}{x} = \dfrac{0 \cdot 5}{2 \cdot 6}$ (c) $\dfrac{x + 3}{3} = \dfrac{5}{4}$ (d) $\dfrac{2}{5} = \dfrac{7}{x + 2}$

3.4 Calculate the length marked x in
this diagram.

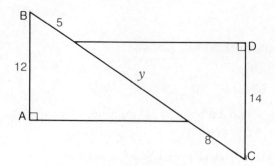

3.5 Calculate the length marked y in this diagram. (AB is parallel to CD.)

4 Saving and borrowing

4.1 Imagine you had a time machine. If you invested £1 in a bank and left it there for 100 years at an annual interest rate of 10% how much would there be in your bank account at the end of the 100 years? With a little thought you shouldn't have to burn your fingers!

4.2 A bank charges 15% per annum to borrow money. If Anita borrowed £1000 at this rate of interest and repaid in two equal yearly instalments, how much would these be?

4.3 There is a rough rule which gives how long it takes a sum of money to double when it is left in the bank at an interest rate of r%. It is:

$$t = \frac{70}{r}$$

where t is the time it takes in years for money, left in the bank at an interest rate of r%, to double. Find how accurate the formula is by calculating, to the nearest year, how long it takes a sum of money to double at an interest rate of

(a) 10% (b) 20% (c) 30%.

5 Area under a graph

5.1 This is part of the graph of the function $r(x) = \frac{1}{x}$.

(a) Calculate the area under the upper step-graph.

(b) Calculate the area under the lower step-graph.

(c) State a reasonable approximation for the area under the curve.

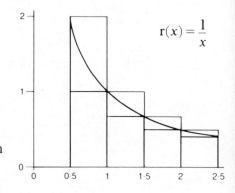

5.2 The diagram below shows the cross-section of a river.
Use the trapezium rule to estimate the area of the cross-section.

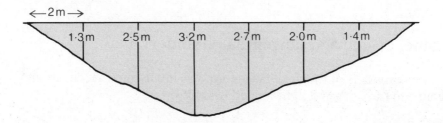

5.3 At a protest march, an observer is estimating the number of people taking part. She counts the number of people who pass her in 1 minute, and does this once every 15 minutes. The march starts at 11 a.m. Here are her results.

Time	11:00	11:15	11:30	11:45	12:00	12:15	12:30	12:45
Rate of passing, in people per minute	120	150	180	190	200	180	140	70

Draw a graph and estimate the total number of people on the march.

6 The trigonometric functions

A Sine, cosine and tangent: a reminder

Here are reminders of the three basic formulas involving sine, cosine and tangent and the sides of a right-angled triangle.

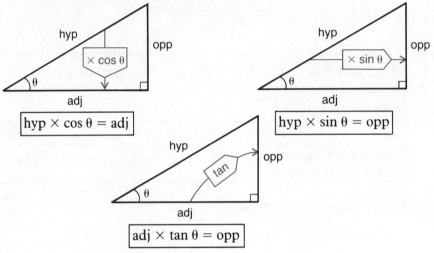

$$\text{hyp} \times \cos \theta = \text{adj}$$

$$\text{hyp} \times \sin \theta = \text{opp}$$

$$\text{adj} \times \tan \theta = \text{opp}$$

A1 Calculate the sides marked with letters in each of these right-angled triangles.

Give each length to the nearest $0 \cdot 1$ cm.

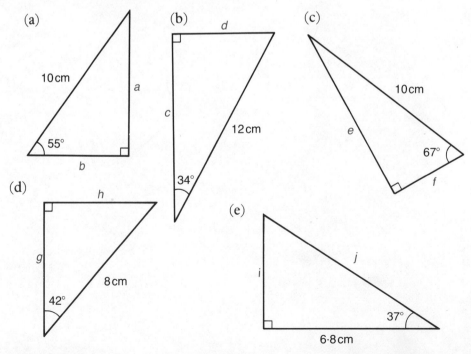

B The unit circle

Although cosine and sine were introduced in connection with
right-angled triangles, they also have a close relationship with
the **circle**, as we shall now see.

This diagram shows the circle whose
centre O is at (0, 0) and whose radius
is 1 unit. We call it the **unit circle**.

Let P be a point on the unit circle.
If we want to tell someone exactly where
P is, we can give the angle between the
positive x-axis and OP.

We shall call this angle θ, and we will
always measure it **anticlockwise**, starting
from the positive x-axis.

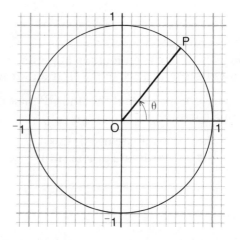

Another way to state the position of P is to give the **coordinates** of P.

If we know the angle θ, we can work out the coordinates of P.

Suppose θ is 50°.

We can use the right-angled triangle shown
in this diagram to find the coordinates of P.

The x-coordinate of P is the side OX which
is adjacent to 50°.
So the x-coordinate of P = hyp × cos 50°
$$= 1 \times \cos 50°$$
$$= \textbf{cos 50°}$$

From a calculator, cos 50° = 0·643 (to 3 d.p.)
and this is the x-coordinate of P.

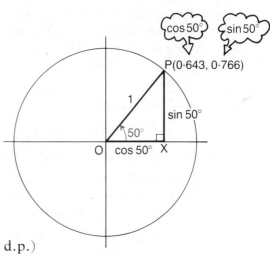

The y-coordinate of P is the side XP which
is opposite 50°.
So the y-coordinate of P = hyp × sin 50°
$$= 1 \times \sin 50°$$
$$= \textbf{sin 50°} = 0·766 \text{ (to 3 d.p.)}$$

B1 Draw a unit circle to a large scale (say 5 cm to 1 unit) on
graph paper. Mark the point P for which the angle θ is 35°.

(a) Use a calculator to find the coordinates of P and check from
your diagram.

(b) Do the same for θ = 75°. Keep the diagram for later.

49

The circle is divided by the *x*- and *y*-axes into four **quadrants**, which are usually numbered anticlockwise as shown here.

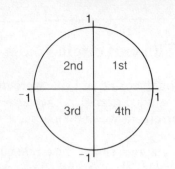

So far we have been looking at points on the unit circle which are in the **first quadrant**.

We have found that if the line OP makes an angle θ with the *x*-axis, then

the *x*-coordinate of P is **cos θ**,
the *y*-coordinate of P is **sin θ**.

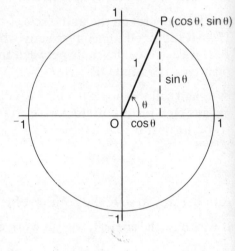

If the angle θ is greater than 90°, then P will be in the 2nd, 3rd or 4th quadrants. We have not yet given any meaning to sines and cosines of angles greater than 90°.
This is because we have used sines and cosines in connection with right-angled triangles, and none of the angles in a right-angled triangle can be more than 90°.

But the unit circle diagram can be used to give meaning to cosines and sines of angles of any size.

We simply say that for **any** angle θ,

cos θ = the *x*-coordinate of P,   sin θ = the *y*-coordinate of P.

For example, when θ = 130°, we find from a calculator that cos 130° = ⁻0·643 (to 3 d.p.) and sin 130° = 0·766 (to 3 d.p.)

(⁻0·643 , 0·766) are the coordinates of P when the angle θ is 130°.

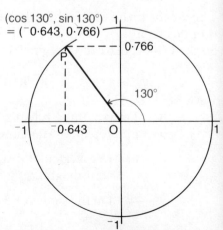

B2   On the diagram for question B1 mark P so that the angle θ is 160°.

Use a calculator to find cos 160° and sin 160° and check that these are the coordinates of P on the diagram.

50

C The sine and cosine functions

The sine of θ is the *y*-coordinate of the point P
on the unit circle.

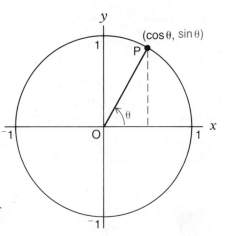

We shall see what happens to sin θ as θ increases
from 0° to 360°.

The diagram below shows the values (to 2 d.p.) of
cos θ and sin θ for angles from 0° to 360° in
steps of 15°.

cos θ is shown in black and sin θ in red.

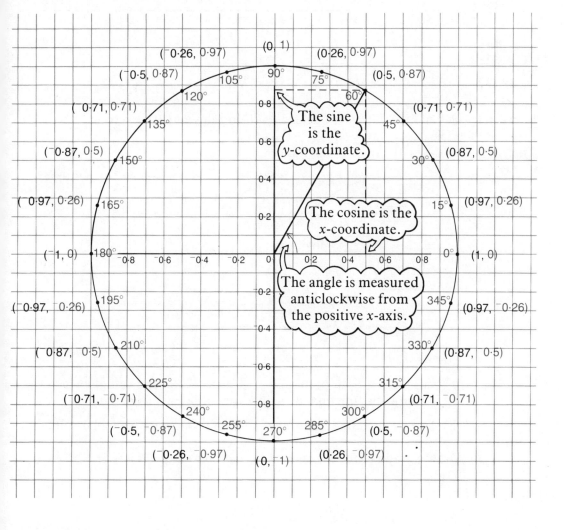

We shall start by looking at the values of sin θ only.

When θ is 0°, sin θ is 0.
As θ goes from 0° to 15°, sin θ increases by 0·26.

As θ goes from 15° to 30°, from 30° to 45°, and so on, sin θ increases
by less and less each time.
Between θ = 75° and θ = 90°, sin θ increases by only 0·03.

This is because of the shape of the circle. The y-coordinate of P
goes up by less and less as P gets towards the top of the circle.

Here is the start of the graph of the function θ → sin θ.

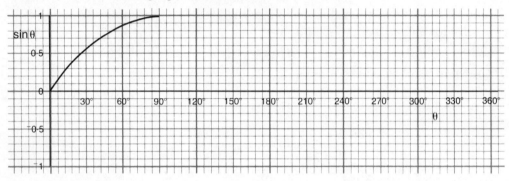

Between θ = 90° and θ = 180°, sin θ decreases from 1 down to 0, slowly at
first and then faster.
The graph continues like this.

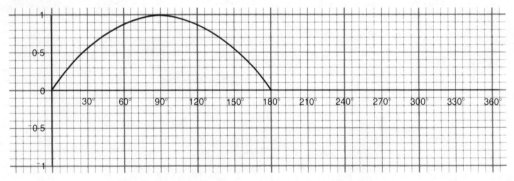

C1 (a) Copy this graph, preferably to a larger scale, and complete it
to show the function θ → sin θ for values of θ from 0° to 360°.

(b) Draw a sketch to show how the graph continues beyond θ = 360°.

C2 Draw a graph of the function θ → cos θ for values of θ from
0° to 360°.

The functions $\theta \rightarrow \sin\theta$ and $\theta \rightarrow \cos\theta$ are **periodic functions**.
Their graphs 'repeat themselves' after every 360°.
We say 360° is the **period** of each of the functions.

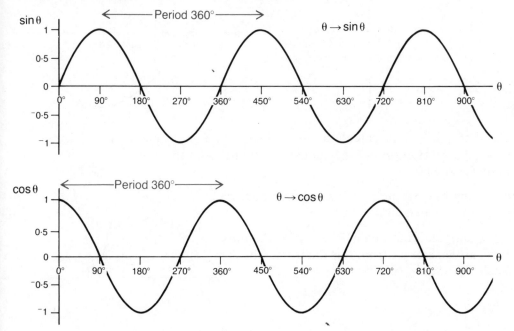

The graph of $\theta \rightarrow \cos\theta$ has the same overall shape as the graph of $\theta \rightarrow \sin\theta$,
but it is shifted 90° to the left.

D Inverse sine

If we use a calculator to find sin 30°, we get sin 30° = 0·5.
0·5 is the sine of 30°, and 30° is the **inverse sine** of 0·5.

We write this inv sin 0·5 = 30°.

If we enter 0·5 on the calculator and press |inv| |sin| (or its equivalent)
we get 30.

But 30° is not the only angle
whose sine is 0·5.

In the range 0° to 360° there are
two angles whose sines are 0·5.

They are 30° and 150°, as you
can see from this diagram.

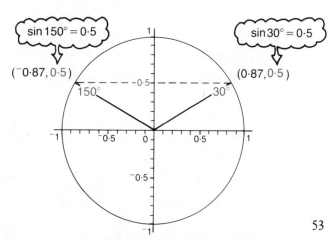

53

You can also see this from the graph of $\theta \to \sin \theta$.

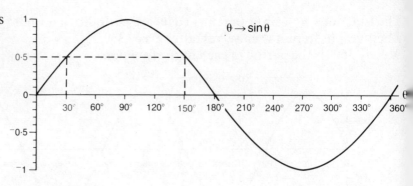

$\theta \to \sin \theta$

Pressing 'inv sin' on the calculator will only give you **one** angle with a given sine. To find the other, you have to think about the circle diagram (or the graph).

The two angles with the same sine are symmetrically placed either side of 90°.

So, for example, if one angle is 75°, the other must be 105°, as you can see from this diagram. Check on a calculator that $\sin 105° = \sin 75°$.

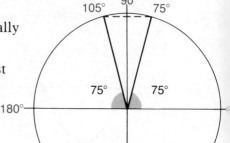

D1 Which other angle in the range 0° to 360° has the same sine as each of these angles? (Sketch a circle diagram to help, if you like.)

(a) 40°   (b) 10°   (c) 115°   (d) 29°   (e) 53·2°   (f) 106·1°

Check each answer by finding sines on a calculator.

D2 (a) Use a calculator to find inv sin 0·3 to the nearest degree.

(b) Write down, to the nearest degree, the other angle in the range 0° to 360° whose sine is also 0·3.

(c) Check on the calculator that the sine of this other angle is the same as that of the first angle.

D3 For each of these equations, find **two** values of θ in the range 0° to 360°. Give each angle to the nearest degree.

(a) $\sin \theta = 0·63$ (b) $\sin \theta = 0·754$ (c) $\sin \theta = 0·209$

D4 Answer this question without looking at any of the diagrams on this page or the opposite page. (Cover them up.)

(a) Which angle in the range 0° to 360° has the same sine as
(i) 37°   (ii) 129°   (iii) 8°   (iv) 52·6°

(b) Find two values of θ in the range 0° to 360° for which $\sin \theta = 0·313$.

54

Suppose you want to know the angles (in the range 0° to 360°) whose sines are both ⁻0·5.

If you use a calculator to find inv sin ⁻0·5, the result will be **⁻30°**.

⁻30° means 30° measured **clockwise** from 0°. So ⁻30° is equivalent to **330°** anticlockwise.

The other angle whose sine is also ⁻0·5 can be found from the circle diagram. It is **210°**.

Check on a calculator that
$\sin 210° = \sin 330° = \sin(^-30°)$.

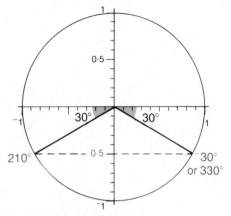

D5 (a) Use a calculator to find inv sin ⁻0·56, to the nearest degree. (The result will be negative.)

(b) Write down, to the nearest degree, two angles in the range 0° to 360° whose sines are both ⁻0·56.

D6 Find two values of θ in the range 0° to 360° for which $\sin θ = ^-0·78$. Give each angle correct to the nearest degree.

D7 For each of these equations, find two values of θ in the range 0° to 360°. Give each angle correct to the nearest degree.

(a) $\sin θ = ^-0·29$ (b) $\sin θ = 0·45$ (c) $\sin θ = ^-0·1$

(d) $\sin θ = 0·1$ (e) $\sin θ = ^-0·9$ (f) $\sin θ = 0·68$

E Inverse cosine

There are two angles in the range 0° to 360° whose cosines are 0·5.

They are 60° and 300°.

This time the two angles are symmetrically placed either side of 0°. (300° is equivalent to ⁻60°.)

If you use a calculator to find inv cos 0·5 you will get the single result 60°.
To get the other angle you have to think about the circle diagram.

Check on a calculator that $\cos 300° = \cos 60°$.

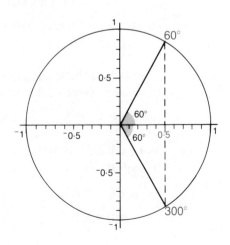

The two angles whose cosines are 0·5 can also be seen from the graph of $\theta \rightarrow \cos\theta$.

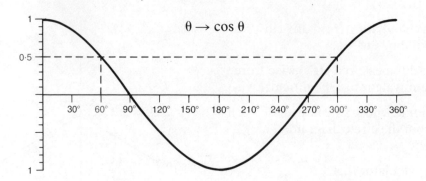

$\theta \rightarrow \cos\theta$

E1 Which other angle in the range 0° to 360° has the same cosine as each of these angles? (Sketch a circle diagram to help, if you like.)

(a) 50°   (b) 45°   (c) 130°   (d) 115°   (e) 240°   (f) 340°

Check each answer by finding the cosines on a calculator.

E2 (a) Use a calculator to find inv cos 0·8, to the nearest degree.

(b) Write down, to the nearest degree, the other angle in the range 0° to 360° whose cosine is also 0·8.

(c) Check on a calculator that the cosine of this other angle is the same as that of the first angle.

E3 For each of these equations, find two values of θ in the range 0° to 360°. Give each angle to the nearest degree.

(a) $\cos\theta = 0\cdot71$ (b) $\cos\theta = 0\cdot326$ (c) $\cos\theta = 0\cdot404$

E4 (a) Which other angle in the range 0° to 360° has the same cosine as 145°? Sketch a circle diagram to help, if you like.

(b) Check on a calculator that the cosines of the two angles are equal.

E5 For each of these equations, find two values of θ in the range 0° to 360°. Give each angle to the nearest degree.

(a) $\cos\theta = {}^-0\cdot5$ (b) $\cos\theta = {}^-0\cdot6$ (c) $\cos\theta = {}^-0\cdot138$

E6 For each equation below, find two values of θ in the range 0° to 360°. Give each angle to the nearest degree.

(a) $\sin\theta = 0\cdot625$ (b) $\sin\theta = {}^-0\cdot833$ (c) $\cos\theta = 0\cdot213$

(d) $\cos\theta = {}^-0\cdot375$ (e) $\sin\theta = 0\cdot208$ (f) $\cos\theta = 0\cdot333$

F The tangent function

The tangent of θ (or tan θ) in the unit circle is $\dfrac{y\text{-coordinate of P}}{x\text{-coordinate of P}}$.

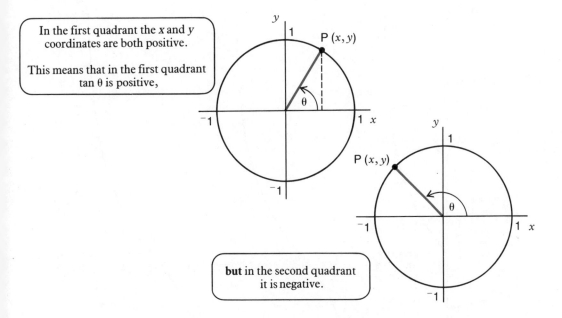

In the first quadrant the x and y coordinates are both positive.

This means that in the first quadrant tan θ is positive,

but in the second quadrant it is negative.

F1 What is the sign of tan θ when the angle θ is in

(a) the third quadrant, (b) the fourth quadrant?

F2 (a) Look carefully at the unit circle, as θ gets closer and closer to 90°. How would you expect tan θ to behave?

(b) What happens when you try to find tan 90° or tan 270° using your calculator?
Discuss with a neighbour why this happens.

F3 Use a calculator to find the tangents of these angles.

(a) 30°   (b) 60°   (c) 120°   (d) 150°

(e) 180°   (f) 210°   (g) 240°   (h) 300°

(i) 330°   (j) 360°

Describe in your own words, using your answers, how the function θ → tan θ behaves for values of θ from 0° to 360°.

F4 Using your calculator as little as possible, make a **rough sketch** of the function θ → tan θ for values of θ from 0° to 360°. Work together with your neighbour for this. Your sketch does not have to be perfect!

Here is a graph of the function $\theta \to \tan \theta$.
As you can see it is entirely different from the functions $\theta \to \cos \theta$
and $\theta \to \sin \theta$.

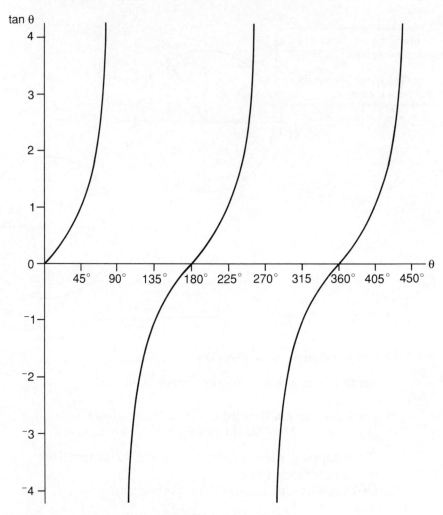

F5 Both $\theta \to \cos \theta$ and $\theta \to \sin \theta$ have a period of 360°.
What is the period of the function $\theta \to \tan \theta$?

What differences can you spot between the functions
$\theta \to \cos \theta$, $\theta \to \sin \theta$ and $\theta \to \tan \theta$?

F6 Ajit is thinking of an angle whose tangent is zero.
Write down at least two angles he may have been
thinking of.

F7 What value do you think $\tan (180n°)$ has
when n is 0, 1, 2, 3, . . .?

G Inverse tangent

Use $\boxed{\text{INV}}$ $\boxed{\text{tan}}$ or $\boxed{\text{tan}^{-1}}$ or their equivalents to find an angle whose tangent is 1.
You should find it to be 45°.

G1 Look at the graph of $\theta \rightarrow \tan \theta$. Find another angle whose tangent is 1.

G2 For each of these equations, find two values of θ in the range 0° to 360°. Give each angle correct to the nearest degree.

(a) $\tan \theta = 2\cdot5$ (b) $\tan \theta = {}^-2\cdot5$ (c) $\tan \theta = 0\cdot65$

(d) $\tan \theta = 50$ (e) $\tan \theta = 0\cdot1$ (f) $\tan \theta = {}^-0\cdot1$

(g) $\tan \theta = {}^-0\cdot01$

Find a connection between the angles in each answer.
Try to explain the connection.

G3 Is this true?

The tangent of double an angle is double the tangent of the angle.

G4 Do any whole-number angles have tangents which are also whole numbers? Investigate for yourselves.

*G5 Explain why there are always two solutions between 0° and 360° for $\tan \theta = a$, where a is any number apart from 0.

*G6 Find the connection between the solutions of $\tan \theta = a$ and $\tan \theta = {}^-a$, where a is any number and θ lies between 0° and 180°.

Graphs and glasses 1

Graphs from pictures

You should work through this with a partner.

When water flows from a tap at a constant rate, the volume of
water in a vase being filled increases at a constant rate.
But how the height of water in the vase changes depends on
the shape of the vase.

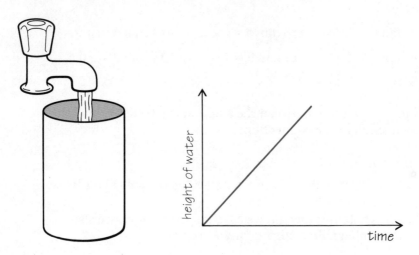

This vase is also filling with water at a constant rate.

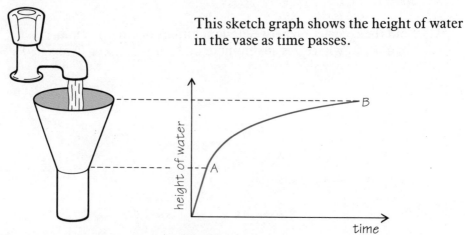

This sketch graph shows the height of water
in the vase as time passes.

Up to A the rate of increase of water height is constant.

From A to B this rate of increase slows down because the vase gets wider.

1   What is happening when the graph becomes horizontal?

2

Sketch the graph that shows
how the height of water changes with
time as this vase is filled.

3 Sketch the graphs you would expect when these vases are filled.

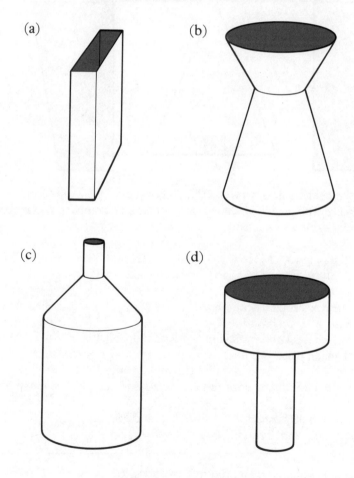

(a) (b)

(c) (d)

4 Draw some graphs for some vases similar in shape to the one in (c),
but larger or smaller in size. What is different about the graphs?
What remains the same?
Choose other vases and see what happens for these.

7 Measuring spread

A What's the difference?

Here is part of a piece of work by some Y9 students.
It is about comparing the strengths of two different brands of spaghetti. They loaded up a scale pan with weights until the piece of spaghetti under test broke.

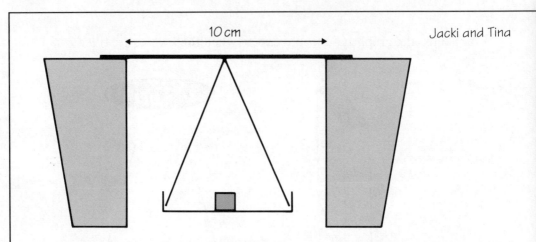

10 cm   Jacki and Tina

We set up the test as it is shown in the diagram and put weights in the pan until the spaghetti broke. The object of the experiment was to compare two different brands of spaghetti. Here are our results.

| Brand A | 18 | 19 | 22 | 15 | 25 | 21 | 22 | 19 | 20 | 19 |
| Brand B | 21 | 21 | 18 | 26 | 12 | 23 | 20 | 17 | 14 | 28 |

Looking at the raw results it was hard to see which of the brands was stronger, so we found the mean of each brand.
For brand A it was 20 and for brand B it was also 20.
This was not much help. The next average we tried was the median.
We put the results in order and found the middle one.
But there was an even number of results so we had to take the mean of the two middle ones.
For brand A it was 19·5 and for brand B it was 20·5.
From this it seems that brand B was the stronger one.

A1 Read through Jacki and Tina's account.

   (a) What very important thing have they missed out?

   (b) Check their working. Do you agree with it?

   (c) Using their figures, compare the two sets of results.
       Do you agree with their conclusion?

A2 Work together to make up different sets of data, each with seven items which have

(a) different means but the same range

(b) the same mean and different ranges

(c) the same mean and the same range

(d) for your results in (c), what is different about your sets of data? If you are not sure make up some more sets of data having the same mean and range and compare them.

A3 Is it possible to have two different sets of data, each having seven items but with the same mean, range and median? Investigate for yourselves.

Mean, mode and median are useful for comparing data but we sometimes need a way of measuring how spread out a set of data is. Range can be used, but sometimes a more sophisticated measure, which uses all the data, is needed.

Here is a possible way with, for example, the data set 0, 1, 2, 3, 3, 4, 4, 4, 5, 5. The mean is $31 \div 10$ which is $3 \cdot 1$.
If we subtract the mean from each item we get:

$^{-}3 \cdot 1, ^{-}2 \cdot 1, ^{-}1 \cdot 1, ^{-}0 \cdot 1, ^{-}0 \cdot 1, 0 \cdot 9, 0 \cdot 9, 0 \cdot 9, 1 \cdot 9, 1 \cdot 9$

Could spread be measured by adding together all these **deviations** from the mean?

Another way could be to add together the differences from the mean.
In other words ignore the signs.
This gives: $3 \cdot 1 + 2 \cdot 1 + 1 \cdot 1 + 0 \cdot 1 + 0 \cdot 1 + 0 \cdot 9 + 0 \cdot 9 + 0 \cdot 9 + 1 \cdot 9 + 1 \cdot 9$
which is 13. This is divided by ten to give $1 \cdot 3$ as a measure of spread.
This is sometimes called the mean difference.

Why is it necessary to divide by the number of pieces of data?

A4 Make up some sets of numbers for yourselves to test the two methods above. Do they both work?

B Standard deviation

Another way of measuring spread is to look at the squares of the differences from the mean. For example, for the set of numbers 2, 3, 3, 5, 5, 7, 7, 8 the mean is 5.

Number	2	3	3	5	5	7	7	8
Difference from the mean (5)	$^-3$	$^-2$	$^-2$	0	0	2	2	3
Difference from the mean squared	9	4	4	0	0	4	4	9

There are eight numbers in the data set.
So the mean value of the differences from the mean squared is
$(9 + 4 + 4 + 0 + 0 + 4 + 4 + 9) \div 8$
$= 34 \div 8 = 4.25$
Before you read on make sure that you understand what is meant by this!
This measure of spread in a set of numbers is called the **variance**.

(The variance is used rather than other measures of spread because it is easier to handle mathematically.)

Statisticians use the square root of the variance as a measure of spread.
This is called the **standard deviation**. In the example above, the standard deviation is $\sqrt{4.25}$ which is approximately 2.6.

B1 Discuss with a partner the probable reason for squaring the deviations.

B2 Here are the points scored by the Jets and the Hawks basketball teams in their last ten games.

Hawks	102	95	103	98	96	96	108	93	115	117
Jets	86	82	90	104	112	114	126	117	109	118

Find the mean and standard deviation of each team's scores.

Which team played the most consistently? Explain your answer.

Your scientific calculator may have special keys which work out the mean and standard deviation directly. Find out how to use yours. To input the raw numbers there is usually a key marked Σ, Σx or SUM. If you've lost your manual, experiment for yourselves! The key which gives the standard deviation for the numbers input is usually marked σ.

B3 Statisticians are sometimes interested in how sensitive statistical measures like variance or standard deviation are. For example, imagine a team that plays very consistently for nine games and then plays really badly for a single game. What difference will it make to the variance and standard deviation? Investigate this problem for yourselves, using these figures as a starting point:

100   101   98   99   102   100   103   99   100   20

Write a short report about your findings. You may need to make up some figures of your own.

B4 Engineers sometimes need to put a number to how rough a surface is. For example, 'B' is obviously rougher than 'A'.
(These sketches are highly magnified cross-sections through surfaces.)

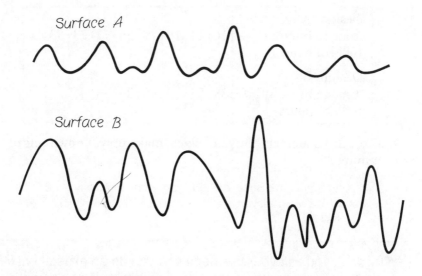

Surface A

Surface B

The problem is how to put a number to roughness.
Can you think of a method? Discuss this with a partner.

B5 The height of ten points picked at random on a surface are measured (in units of 0·01 mm). They are: 180, 175, 90, 120, 95, 75, 65, 90, 110, 70.
By mistake Amy added 100 units to each of these results.
Will this affect the value of the variance for these ten heights?

B6

Spacecraft keep oxygen and other gases stored under pressure in cylinders. It is very important that these cylinders are strong enough. Cylinders are tested by filling them with gas to ten times the normal pressure and seeing how long (measured in hundreds of hours) it is until they burst.

Here are the bursting times for two different cylinder designs.
Write a short report suggesting which is the safer design.
Give reasons for your decision.

Design 'A' (time to burst in 100's of hours)	10	14	19	79	56	13	23	83	1
Design 'B' (time to burst in 100's of hours)	38	54	19	40	24	23	45		

B7 Test this statement for yourselves, make up your own sets of numbers.

The mean difference is equal, very approximately, to 0·8 times the standard deviation. This is a useful quick check.

Why don't you ask your teacher if you can do an experiment like Jacki and Tina's spaghetti testing? Use standard deviations in your conclusions.

C Using grouped data

Suppose you need to find the mean for some grouped data like this:

Height of tree (h) in metres	$0.5 \leq h < 1.5$	$1.5 \leq h < 2.5$	$2.5 \leq h < 3.5$	$3.5 \leq h < 4.5$	$4.5 \leq h < 5.5$
Frequency	4	1	17	22	6

You need to assume that the sum of the data in an interval is equal to the half-way point of the interval (the mid-interval) multiplied by the number of items of data in the interval – like this:

Height of tree (h) in metres	$0.5 \leq h < 1.5$	$1.5 \leq h < 2.5$	$2.5 \leq h < 3.5$	$3.5 \leq h < 4.5$	$4.5 \leq h < 5.5$
Frequency	4	1	17	22	6
Mid-interval	1	2	3	4	5
Freq. × mid-interval	4	2	51	88	30

The **estimated** mean tree height for this data is:

$$\frac{4 + 2 + 51 + 88 + 30}{4 + 1 + 17 + 22 + 6} = \frac{175}{50}$$
$$= 3.5 \text{ metres}$$

The variance and standard deviation are worked out in a similar way.

C1 Find the variance and standard deviation of this grouped data.
You must talk this through together.
(The variance is 1.01, but it's the method that counts.)

C2 What happens to the estimated mean and standard deviation if you use intervals which are twice as large? For example $0.5 \leq h < 2.5$, $2.5 \leq h < 4.5$ and $4.5 \leq h < 6.5$.

C3 It is important that chemical laboratories are consistent when they analyse chemicals. Here are the results of the analysis of the percentage calcium found in some samples taken from the same flask. The two laboratories each analysed twenty samples.

Laboratory A

2·48	2·79	3·65	3·16	2·53	2·96	2·65	2·95	2·80	3·24
2·91	3·04	3·77	3·08	2·68	3·62	2·89	3·25	3·07	3·31

Laboratory B

2·59	2·97	3·08	3·39	3·33	3·17	2·96	2·54	2·64	2·96
3·64	2·72	2·73	2·98	3·11	3·45	3·48	3·19	2·96	3·18

Show these results on a grouped frequency table.
Which is the most consistent laboratory?
Back your answer up with some figures.

The symbol σ (sigma) is used for standard deviation. You may have noticed the σ key on your calculator. Wherever your data comes from, on average, at least 75% of them will be within 2σ (two standard deviations of the estimated mean).

C4 Here is a grouped frequency table for 243 cuckoo eggs.

Length (L mm)	Number	Breadth (B mm)	Number
$18·75 \leq L < 19·25$	1	$13·75 \leq B < 14·25$	1
$19·25 \leq L < 19·75$	1	$14·25 \leq B < 14·75$	1
$19·75 \leq L < 20·25$	7	$14·75 \leq B < 15·25$	5
$20·25 \leq L < 20·75$	3	$15·25 \leq B < 15·75$	9
$20·75 \leq L < 21·25$	29	$15·75 \leq B < 16·25$	73
$21·25 \leq L < 21·75$	13	$16·25 \leq B < 16·75$	51
$21·75 \leq L < 22·25$	54	$16·75 \leq B < 17·25$	80
$22·25 \leq L < 22·75$	38	$17·25 \leq B < 17·75$	15
$22·75 \leq L < 23·25$	47	$17·75 \leq B < 18·25$	7
$23·25 \leq L < 23·75$	22	$18·25 \leq B < 18·75$	0
$23·75 \leq L < 24·25$	21	$18·75 \leq B < 19·25$	1
$24·25 \leq L < 24·75$	5		
$24·75 \leq L < 25·25$	2		
Total	243	Total	243

(a) Use graphs, and anything else you think is suitable, to make a report summarising the above data.

(b) Does the '2σ rule' fit this data?

Back of an envelope 2

1 Here are some more calculations scribbled on the back of an envelope. The symbol ≈ (or sometimes ≏) means approximately equal to. Try to follow the working.

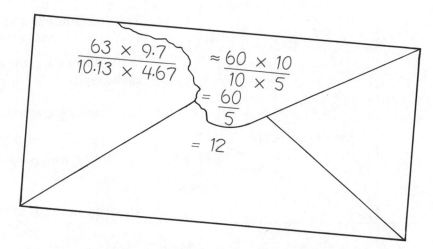

$$\frac{63 \times 9.7}{10.13 \times 4.67} \approx \frac{60 \times 10}{10 \times 5}$$
$$= \frac{60}{5}$$
$$= 12$$

How close is the approximation to the 'true' answer?

Approximate answers should be used to check that answers to calculations are reasonable.

2 Check these using approximations. Show your working as in the example above. When you have finished compare your working and answers with a partner.

(a) $(0.25 \times 81.1) \div 5.7 = 35.57018$

(b) $6.8 \times \cos 2° = 7.8641$

(c) $\dfrac{7.7 \times 83 \times 79}{3.5 \times 6} = 2339.90384$

(d) $23 \times \sqrt{103.5} = 331.99038$

3 Find approximate answers to these:

(a) $(201 \div 2) \times 69.159$

(b) $\sqrt{143.5} \div 1.698$

(c) $\dfrac{3674}{(295 + 0.1)}$

(d) $\dfrac{5012.56}{\sqrt{3} + 468}$

4 A rough calculation can tell you if an answer is wrong, but can it tell you if it is correct?

69

8 Equations and graphs

A The graph of $y = ax$

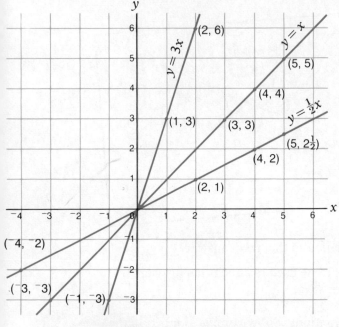

A1 The diagram shows the graphs of $y = 3x$, $y = x$ and $y = \frac{1}{2}x$.

Write down the gradient of each graph.

A2 (a) Draw the graphs of
        (i) $y = 2x$ (ii) $y = {}^-3x$

    (b) Write down the gradient of each graph.

A3 Describe in words the graph of
    (a) $y = 100x$ (b) $y = {}^-100x$

A4 Explain why the graph of $y = ax$ goes through $(0, 0)$, whatever the value of a.

The graph of $y = ax$ is a straight line through $(0, 0)$ with gradient a.

If a is positive, the line slopes upwards from left to right.

If a is negative, the line slopes downwards from left to right.

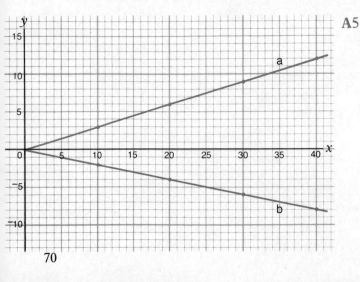

A5 (a) Find the gradient of each of these graphs.

    (b) Write down the equation of each graph.

B The graph of $y = ax + b$

> The use of a graphical calculator or graph-plotting software is recommended for this section.

Here is the graph of $y = \frac{1}{2}x$.

If we change the equation to $y = \frac{1}{2}x + 2$, every point on $y = \frac{1}{2}x$ moves up 2 units.

The **intercept** on the y-axis is now **2**. The gradient is still $\frac{1}{2}$.

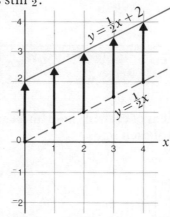

If we change the equation to $y = \frac{1}{2}x - 2$, every point on $y = \frac{1}{2}x$ moves down 2 units.

The intercept on the y-axis is now ⁻2. The gradient is still $\frac{1}{2}$.

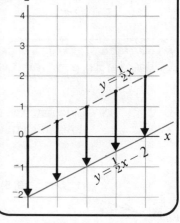

B1 Experiment with different values of b in $y = \frac{1}{2}x + b$. How do different values of b affect the line?

B2 How do different values of b in $y = -\frac{1}{2}x + b$ affect the straight line?

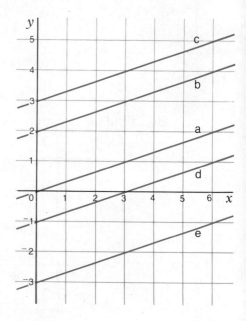

B3 All of the lines in the diagram on the right have a gradient of $\frac{1}{3}$.

For each line, write down

(i) its intercept on the y-axis

(ii) its equation

71

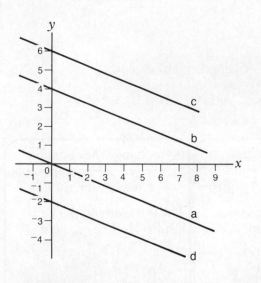

B4 All the lines in the diagram on the left have gradient ⁻0·4.

Write down the equation of each line.

> The graph of $y = ax + b$ is a straight line of gradient a,
> whose intercept on the y-axis is b.

B5 Calculate the gradient of each of these lines, and write down the equation of each line.

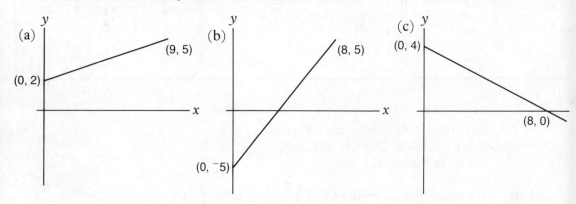

(a)

(0, 2)

(9, 5)

(b)

(0, ⁻5)

(8, 5)

(c)

(0, 4)

(8, 0)

B6 Find the equation of each of these lines.

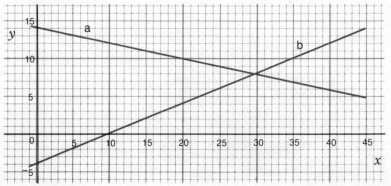

a

b

72

C The graphs of $y = ax^2$, $y = ax^3$ and $y = \frac{a}{x}$

C1 Draw axes on graph paper, with x from $^-2$ to 2 and y from $^-2$ to 6.

Here is a table of values for the equation $y = x^2$.

x	$^-2$	$^-1{\cdot}5$	$^-1$	$^-0{\cdot}5$	0	0·5	1	1·5	2
y	4	2·25	1	0·25	0	0·25	1	2·25	4

(a) Draw the graph of $y = x^2$ and label it.

(b) The graph of $y = 1 \cdot 5x^2$ can be drawn on the same axes.
To do this you need to multiply all the values of y in the table by 1·5. Draw the graph of $y = 1 \cdot 5x^2$.

(c) Now draw the graph of $y = {}^-0 \cdot 5x^2$ on the same set of axes.

The graphs you drew in question C1 show the general shape of the graph of $y = ax^2$.

The graph of $y = ax^2$ is a curve which touches the x-axis at $(0, 0)$ and gets steeper and steeper further away from $(0, 0)$.

The graph of $y = ax^2$

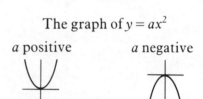

a positive   a negative

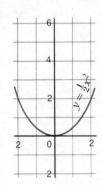

C2 This is a sketch of the graph of $y = \frac{1}{2}x^2$.

Copy the sketch and add to it the graphs of $y = \frac{1}{2}x^2 + 3$ and $y = \frac{1}{2}x^2 - 2$, showing clearly how they are related to the graph of $y = \frac{1}{2}x^2$.

C3 Use your graphical calculator or software to investigate what happens for different values of a and b in $y = ax^2 + b$.
Make a note of anything interesting you find.

C4 Draw axes on graph paper with x from $^-2$ to 2 and y from $^-12$ to 12.
Here is a table of values for the equation $y = x^3$.

x	$^-2{\cdot}0$	$^-1{\cdot}5$	$^-1{\cdot}0$	$^-0{\cdot}5$	0	0·5	1·0	1·5	2·0
y	$^-8$	$^-3{\cdot}375$	$^-1$	$^-0{\cdot}125$	0	0·125	1	3·375	8

(a) Draw the graph of $y = x^3$ and label it.

(b) The graph of $y = 1 \cdot 5x^3$ can be drawn quite easily. All you need to do is to multiply all the values of y in the table by 1·5. Draw the graph of $y = 1 \cdot 5x^3$.

(c) Draw the graph of $y = {}^-0 \cdot 5x^3$ on the same axes.

73

C5 The graphs you drew in **C4** show the general shape of the graph $y = ax^3$. Use your graphical calculator or software to investigate what effect changing the value of a has on the graph.

The graph $y = ax^3$ is a curve which passes through the origin $(0, 0)$ and gets steeper the further away it is from the origin. Look at the small diagrams to see the difference when a is positive or negative.

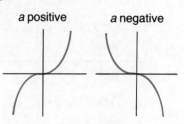

a positive   a negative

C6

This is a sketch of the graph $y = 0{\cdot}5x^3$. Copy the sketch and add to it the graphs of $y = 0{\cdot}5x^3 + 3$ and $y = 0{\cdot}5x^3 - 2$. How are these two graphs related to the graph of $y = 0{\cdot}5x^3$?

C7 Use your graphical calculator or software to investigate what effect different values of a and b have on the graph of $y = ax^3 + b$.

C8 Draw axes on graph paper with x and y from $^-6$ to 6.

(a) Calculate the value of y when x is 6, 5, 4, 3, 2, 1·5, 1 and 0·5, for $y = \dfrac{3}{x}$ and make a table of values.

(b) Why is there no value of y when x is 0?

(c) Continue the table of values to show the value of y when x is $^-0{\cdot}5$, $^-1$, $^-1{\cdot}5$, $^-2$, $^-3$, $^-4$, $^-5$ and $^-6$.

(d) Draw the graph of $y = \dfrac{3}{x}$.

This diagram shows the graphs of $y = \dfrac{3}{x}$ and $y = \dfrac{12}{x}$.

Each graph is in two parts.

As x increases, the graphs get closer and closer to the x-axis, but never reach it.

Other graphs of the form $y = \dfrac{a}{x}$ have the same kind of shape. If a is negative, the graph occupies the other two 'quadrants', like this.

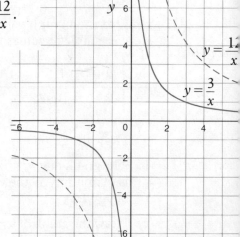

$y = \dfrac{12}{x}$

$y = \dfrac{3}{x}$

74

C9 Investigate with your graphical calculator or software the effect of changing the value of a in $y = \dfrac{a}{x}$.

C10 A girl was asked to draw sketch graphs of these equations:

$$y = 2 - 0{\cdot}8x^3 \qquad y = 0{\cdot}8x^3 \qquad y = \dfrac{^-2}{x} \qquad y = {}^-0{\cdot}8x^3$$

$$y = 2{\cdot}5x \qquad y = 0{\cdot}8x \qquad y = 1{\cdot}5x - 2 \qquad y = 4 - 0{\cdot}6x$$

$$y = 0{\cdot}8x^2 \qquad y = 0{\cdot}3x^2 + 4 \qquad y = 4 - 0{\cdot}3x^2 \qquad y = \dfrac{2}{x}$$

She drew them all correctly, but forgot to label them. Which of the equations goes with each graph?

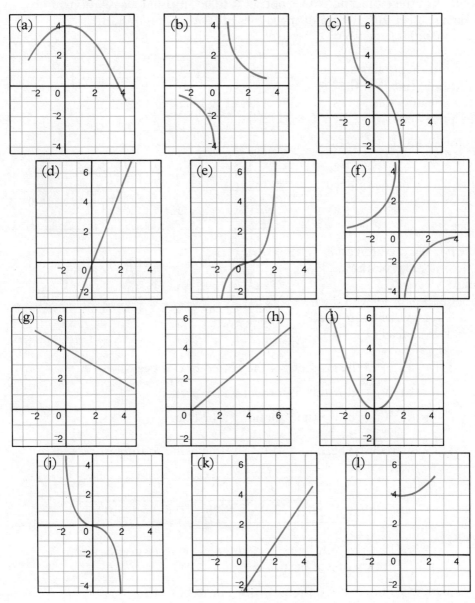

D Fitting a linear equation

The use of a graphical calculator or software which has a 'line of best fit' option is recommended for this section.

In a chemistry experiment, potassium bromide was dissolved in 100g of water at 0°C. The mass which could be dissolved was measured. Then the experiment was repeated at various different temperatures. These were the results.

t	0	19	41	60	80
m	53·4	64·1	75·2	84·7	95·5

t stands for the temperature in °
and m for the mass in grams
which could be dissolved.

If we look at the table, there does not seem to be any obvious relationship between t and m. But if we plot the values of (t, m) on a graph, then a relationship is suggested.

The points do not lie exactly on a straight line, but the dotted line drawn here fits them quite well.

The dotted line is a 'line of best fit'.

The equation of the line will be of the form

$m = at + b$

where a is the gradient and b is the intercept on the m-axis.
(The equation is derived from $y = ax + b$ by writing t instead of x, and m instead of y.)

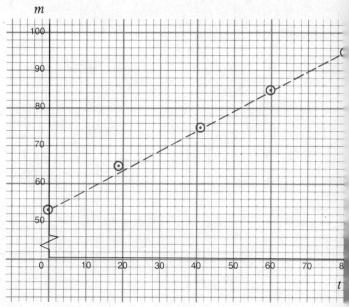

D1 (a) Find the gradient of the dotted line of best fit.

(b) Write down its intercept on the y-axis.

(c) Write down the equation of the line.

D2 A similar experiment, but this time using sodium nitrate, gave these results.

t	0	20	32	40
m	72·9	87·5	96·3	102

(a) Plot the four pairs of values of (t, m) on a graph, and draw a line of best fit.

(b) Find the equation of your line of best fit.

76

D3 This table shows pairs of measurements of two variables p and q.

p	12·0	15·3	17·8	19·0
q	24·4	29·0	32·6	34·2

(a) Plot the four points on a (p, q) graph and draw a line of best fit.

(b) Find the equation of your line of best fit.

D4 Repeat question D3 for this table.

p	50·0	62·4	80·5	97·0
q	7·50	6·50	5·05	3·75

E Fitting other equations

Suppose we use the method described in the previous section to the data in this table.

p	1·3	1·9	2·5	3·1	3·8	4·4
q	14·6	18·5	23·7	30·5	40·1	50·0

We start by drawing the graph of (p, q).

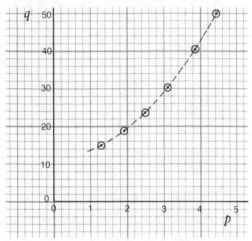

This time the graph is not a straight line.
It curves upwards, getting steeper and steeper, and this suggests an equation with p^2 in it.

It can't be of the form $q = ap^2$, because that would go through $(0, 0)$, . . .

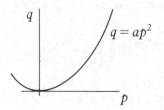

but it might be of the form $q = ap^2 + b$.

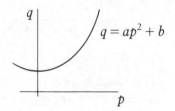

There is a method of 'transforming' a graph of the form $q = ap^2 + b$ into a straight-line graph.

We first compare the equation $q = ap^2 + b$ with the standard straight-line equation $y = ax + b$:

$$q = a\,p^2 + b$$
$$\downarrow \quad \downarrow$$
$$y = a\,x + b$$

We let x be p^2, and y be q. We make a new table of values.

$x(=p^2)$	1·69	3·61	6·25	9·61	14·44	19·36
$y(=q)$	14·6	18·5	23·7	30·5	40·1	50·0

These are the squares of the values of p in the original table.

Now we draw the graph of (x, y), with a line of best fit.

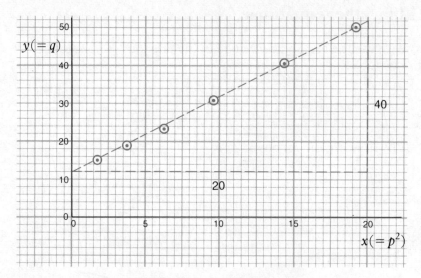

As before, we find the gradient and intercept of this line.
Its gradient is $\frac{40}{20} = 2$. The intercept on the y-axis is **12**.

So the equation of the line is $y = 2x + 12$.

Now remember that x stands for p^2 and y stands for q; so the equation connecting q and p is

$$q = 2p^2 + 12.$$

E1 This table shows pairs of values of two variables p and q.

p	3·0	4·6	5·2	6·0	7·4
q	24·5	30·6	33·5	38·0	47·4

It is thought that there is a relationship between p and q, of the form $q = ap^2 + b$. Let x be p^2 and y be q; make a table of values of (x, y), draw a graph and use it to find a and b.

78

E2 Two variables S and T are believed to be related by an equation of the form $T = aS^2 + b$.

Here are some pairs of values of S and T.

S	1·5	2·5	3·0	4·0	4·5
T	31·6	25·6	21·5	11·0	4·6

By drawing a suitable graph, find the values of a and b.

The method can be extended to other kinds of relationship.

Suppose p and q are connected by an equation of the form $q = ap^3 + b$. We compare this equation with the standard straight-line equation.

$$q = ap^3 + b$$
$$\downarrow \qquad \downarrow$$
$$y = ax + b$$

This tells us to let x be p^3, and y be q. We will then get a straight-line graph from which we can find the values of a and b.

If the equation connecting p and q is of the form $q = a\sqrt{p} + b$, we would let x be $\sqrt{p}$ and y be q.

If the equation is of the form $q = \dfrac{a}{p} + b$, or $q = a\left(\dfrac{1}{p}\right) + b$, we would let x be $\dfrac{1}{p}$ and y be q.

E3 Two variables p and q are connected by an equation of the form $q = a\sqrt{p} + b$. Here are some pairs of values of p and q.

p	1·4	3·3	7·2	10·6	15·8
q	11·5	13·0	15·2	16·6	18·4

(a) Let $x = \sqrt{p}$ and $y = q$. Make a table of values of x and y.

(b) Draw the graph of (x, y) and use it to find the values of a and b.

(c) Check that the equation $q = a\sqrt{p} + b$ fits the numbers in the original table.

E4 Two variables R and S are connected by an equation of the form $S = \dfrac{a}{R} + b$.

Here are some values of R and S.

R	1·2	1·5	2·0	2·5	3·0
S	6·4	4·4	2·4	1·2	0·4

By drawing a suitable graph, find the values of a and b.

9 Three dimensions

A Orthographic projections

Orthographic projections are used a great deal by architects, designers and engineers. This is because it is possible to take accurate measurements from orthographic projections.

Usually, three orthographic projections of an object are enough to give a 'total picture' of it.

They are called a **plan** (from above) and **elevations** (usually from the front and side).

Orthographic projections are often called 'views'.

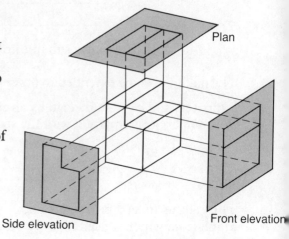

Plan

Side elevation

Front elevation

A1 Here are a plan and two elevations of a shed, drawn to a scale of 1 cm to 1 m.

The roof (shaded) is covered with roofing felt.

A
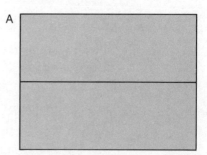

B
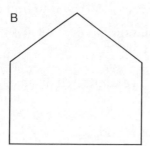

C
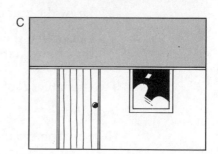

(a) Which of the three views, A, B, C could be used to measure the height of the shed?

(b) Calculate the area of the roofing felt. Explain carefully how you do it.

A2 Here are three full-size orthographic
projections of a 3-pin plug.

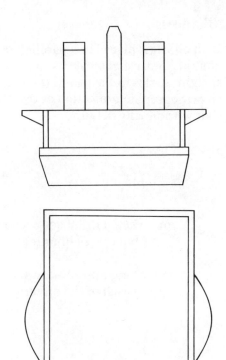

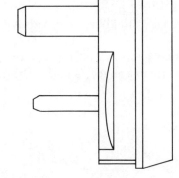

(a) The diagram on the left shows a socket which the plug
will fit. What are the full-size measurements a, b, c, d?

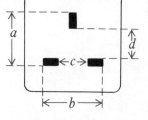

(b) The diagram on the right shows a
double socket into which two of the
plugs will fit.
What is the smallest that e can be?

Dotted lines are often used to show features
which are out of sight. For example,
here are two views of a hollow cylinder.

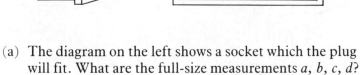

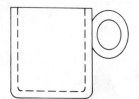

A3 This is a side view of an object.
Sketch a plan view.

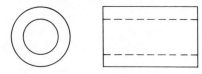

'Shadows'

If an object is placed in a parallel beam
of light, and a shadow is cast on a plane
at right-angles to the beam, the shadow is
an orthographic projection of the object
(but without any detail).

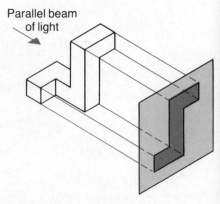

Parallel beam
of light

A4 Sketch the shadow you would get if the object in the diagram
above were illuminated by a parallel beam from above.

A5 Sketch the shadows obtained by illuminating each of these objects
in each of the directions A (from above), B and C (horizontally).

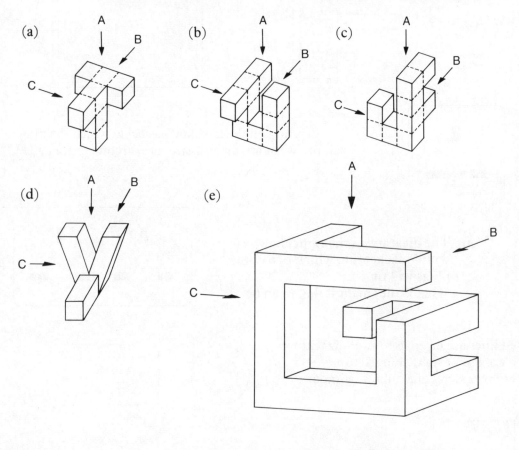

(a)

(b)

(c)

(d)

(e)

A6 Sketch a single object which
can give these three shadows.

B Other kinds of projection

Perspective views show objects as they really appear, but they are difficult to draw accurately.

Orthogonal projections are easier to draw, but you need several different views of an object to get a 'total picture'.

There are other ways of representing three-dimensional objects in two-dimensional drawings. Here we show a matchbox drawn in three different ways.

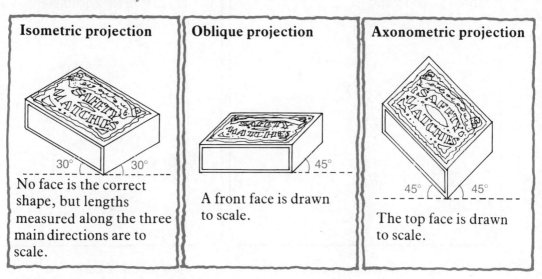

Isometric projection

No face is the correct shape, but lengths measured along the three main directions are to scale.

Oblique projection

A front face is drawn to scale.

Axonometric projection

The top face is drawn to scale.

Axonometric projection is often used in architecture.
Measurements of the plan of a building can be made from an axonometric drawing.

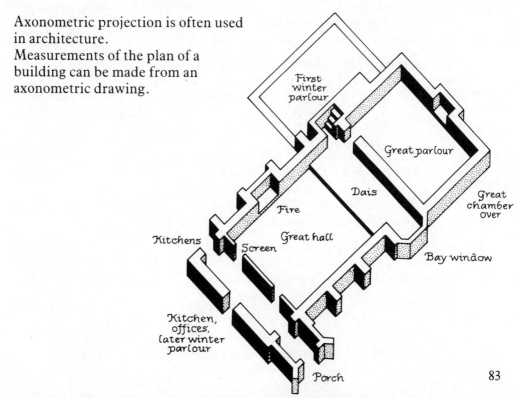

First winter parlour

Great parlour

Dais

Great chamber over

Fire

Kitchens

Screen

Great hall

Bay window

Kitchen, offices, later winter parlour

Porch

C Coordinates in three dimensions

So far in this chapter we have looked at ways of representing objects
in three-dimensional space by two-dimensional drawings.

Another way to represent three-dimensional space is by numbers.

In two dimensions, we can represent the
position of a point by two **coordinates**,
which we call x and y.

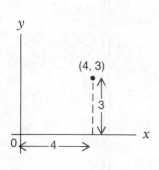

In three dimensions, we need three
coordinates to give the position of a poi
We call the three coordinates x, y and z

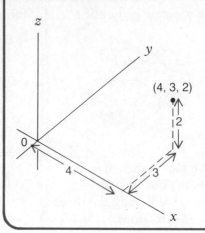

It often helps to think of the plane containing the x- and y-axes
as a horizontal plane. The z-coordinate then tells us how far a point
is above (or below) the 'xy'-plane. So if a point is actually in the xy-plane,
its z-coordinate is 0.

For example, at the point C in this diagram,
the x-coordinate is 3 and the y-coordinate is 3.
The z-coordinate at C is 0, so C is $(3, 3, 0)$.

G is 3 units above C, so G is $(3, 3, 3)$.

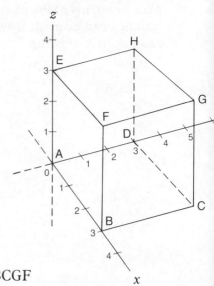

C1 Write down the coordinates of
A, B, C, D, E, F, G, and H.

C2 Write down the coordinates
of the midpoint of

(a) EH   (b) FG   (c) AC

C3 Write down the coordinates
of the centre of the face

(a) ABFE   (b) DCGH   (c) BCGF

C4 Write down the coordinates of the centre of the cube.

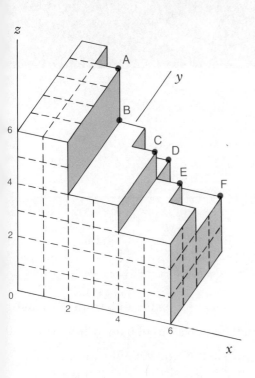

C5 Write down the coordinates of the points marked A to F in the diagram on the left.

C6 Calculate the lengths PQ, QR and PR in the diagram below.

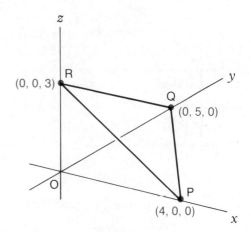

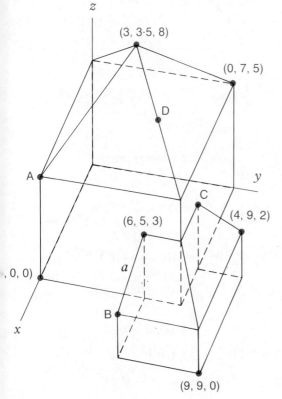

C7 The diagram on the left shows a house with an extension.

(a) Write down the coordinates of the points marked A, B and C.

(b) D is the midpoint of a sloping edge of the roof of the house. Work out the coordinates of D.

(c) The measurements are all in metres. Calculate the length of the sloping edge a of the extension roof.

(d) Calculate the angle the edge a makes with the horizontal.

(e) Calculate the length of each of the four sloping edges of the roof of the house.

85

Review 2

6 The trigonometric functions

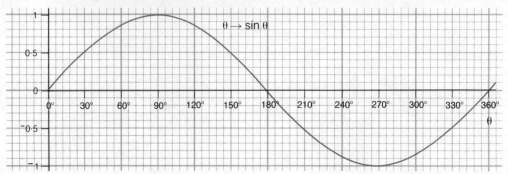

6.1 This is the graph of the function $\theta \rightarrow \sin \theta$ for values of θ from $0°$ to $360°$.

(a) From the graph find approximately the values of θ for which $\sin \theta = 0$

(b) If you use a calculator to find inv sin 0·6 you get only one angle, $36·9°$ (to 1 d.p.). What is the other angle, also correct to 1 d.p.?

6.2 Copy this sketch of the graph of $\theta \rightarrow \sin \theta$, and sketch on the same axes the graph of $\theta \rightarrow \cos \theta$. Label both graphs.

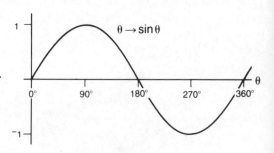

6.3 Find two angles in the range $0°$ to $360°$ whose cosines are $0·75$. Give each answer to the nearest degree.

6.4 Find, to the nearest degree, two angles in the range $0°$ to $360°$ whose sines are $0·25$.

6.5 Find two angles in the range $0°$ to $360°$ whose tangents are $1·5$.

6.6 Find two values of θ in the range $0°$ to $360°$ which satisfy each of these equations.

(a) $\sin \theta = 0·44$ (b) $\cos \theta = 0·69$ (c) $\tan \theta = 0·65$

(d) $\cos \theta = {}^-0·83$ (e) $\cos \theta = 0·09$ (f) $\tan \theta = {}^-4$

(g) $\sin \theta = 0·09$ (h) $\sin \theta = {}^-0·09$ (i) $\tan \theta = 0·21$

7 Measuring spread

7.1 Here are the times in seconds for two 400 metre runners.
Who is the more consistent runner? Give reasons for your answer.

Meena	65	61	67	66	71	65	67
Reva	63	61	66	64	69	68	71

7.2 These figures show the Vickers pyramid hardness number (h) of some metal samples. (Hardness is worked out from the dent made by a sharp pyramid-shaped point.)

Vickers hardness number (h)	$92 \leq h < 96$	$96 \leq h < 100$	$100 \leq h < 104$	$104 \leq h < 108$	$108 \leq h < 112$	$112 \leq h < 116$
Frequency	1	9	21	18	7	1

(a) Find the standard deviation and mean of these figures.

(b) About how many of the hardness readings are within one standard deviation of the estimated mean?

8 Equations and graphs

8.1 (a) What is the gradient of line a in this diagram?

(b) Write down the equation of line a.

(c) Write down the equation of line b.

(d) Write down the equation of line c.

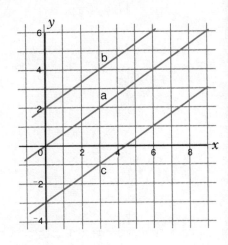

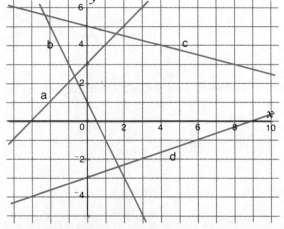

8.2 Write down

(i) the gradient

(ii) the intercept on the y-axis

(iii) the equation

of each line shown in this diagram.

87

8.3 Diagrams A to L below are rough sketches of the graphs of the following equations:

$$y = 2 + \tfrac{1}{2}x \qquad y = 2 - \tfrac{1}{2}x \qquad y = \tfrac{1}{2}x - 2 \qquad y = \tfrac{1}{2}x^3$$

$$y = 2x^2 \qquad y = 2 + x^2 \qquad y = 2 - x^2 \qquad y = x^2 - 2$$

$$y = \frac{2}{x} \qquad\qquad y = \frac{-2}{x} \qquad\qquad y = 2 - 2x \qquad y = 2 - \tfrac{1}{2}x^3$$

Match the correct equation to each sketch.

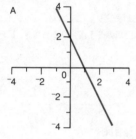 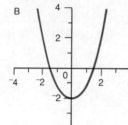 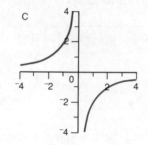 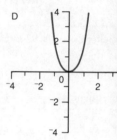

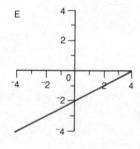 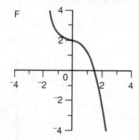 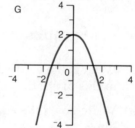 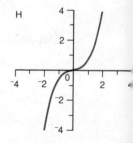

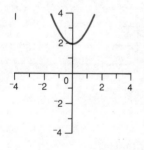 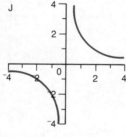 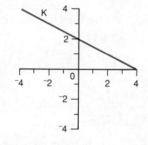 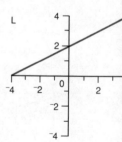

8.4 The following data is believed to fit approximately an equation of the form $Q = aP + b$.

P	4·0	5·8	6·9	8·8	10·0
Q	15·6	14·7	14·0	13·0	12·2

Draw a line of best fit and use it to find values for a and b.

8.5 The following data is believed to fit approximately an equation of the form $v = au^2 + b$.

u	0·7	1·2	2·2	2·6	3·0	3·5
v	⁻4·3	⁻2·8	2·3	5·1	8·5	13·4

Draw a suitable straight-line graph and use it to find values for a and b.

9 Three dimensions

9.1 These drawings show a front elevation and a side elevation of a workshop. They are drawn to a scale of 1 cm to 1 m.

 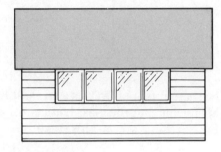

(a) Find the area of the floor of the workshop.

(b) The roof is covered with roofing felt. Find the area of the roofing felt.

9.2 Draw full-size a plan view, a front elevation and a left-side elevation of the solid shown here.

(All measurements are in mm.)

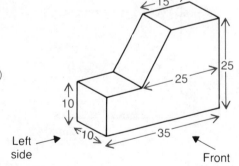

9.3 One edge of a cuboid is from $(0, 0, 0)$ to $(2, 0, 0)$. Another is from $(0, 0, 0)$ to $(0, 4, 0)$. Another is from $(0, 0, 0)$ to $(0, 0, 5)$. Write down the coordinates of the other four corners of the cuboid.

Graphs and glasses 2

Pictures from graphs

This graph shows the depth of water of a glass filled from a tap.
The water in the tap comes out at a constant rate.

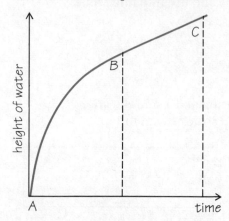

The section from A to B is curved.

This shows that the rate of increase of depth is changing.

In fact it is slowing down.

This means that the cross-sectional area is increasing the further up the glass you go.

The section from B to C is a straight line. This means that the glass has a constant cross-sectional area at this stage.

This could be the shape of the glass.

1   Which of these sketch graphs might show a glass which is overflowing?

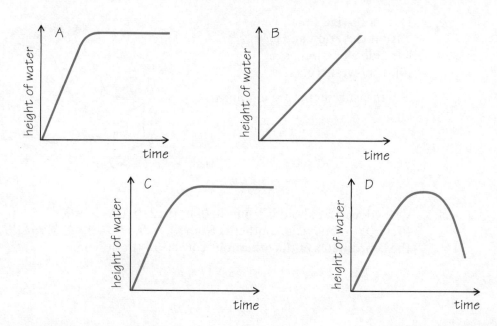

2 Match each of these sketch graphs to a glass or glasses.

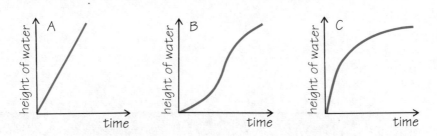

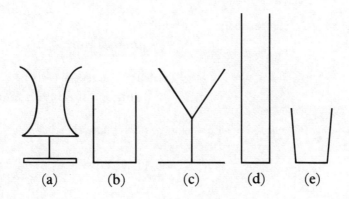

(a) (b) (c) (d) (e)

3 Draw some glasses which could fit these sketch graphs.

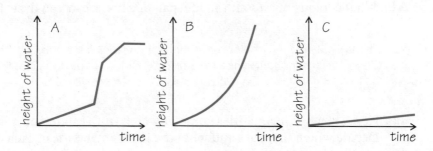

4 Is this true?

'Providing all parts of the graph slope upwards to the right, you can always draw a glass which fits.'

10 Inequations

A Inequalities

> ### Reminder
>
> You have probably seen expressions like these before:
>
> Store at a **temperature** less than 3°C.
>
> $$[\textbf{temperature} < 3\,°C]$$
>
> 6th form students must study at least 2 **A levels**.
>
> $$[\text{number of } \textbf{A levels} \text{ studied} \geq 2]$$
>
> When you throw an ordinary dice you can **score** any number from 1 to 6.
>
> $$[1 \leq \textbf{score} \leq 6]$$

A1 What conclusions about the lifespan of a horse can you draw from this?

The typical lifespan of a horse is more than twice that of a dog. Dogs live longer than either cows or pigs. But cows outlive pigs by at least eight years. On average a pig lives for ten years.

A2 Here are a few inequalities **some** of which fit the statements in **A1**. Decide which these are and what the letters stand for in each case.

(a) $a \leq b + c$ (b) $d > 2e$ (c) $2e > d$ (d) $f < g + 8$

(e) $g + 8 \leq f$ (f) $h < i$ (g) $j > k$

Discuss your answers with a partner.

A3 Copy and complete each of these, replacing ✶ by $=$, $>$ or $<$.

(a) $(0{\cdot}01)^2$ ✶ $0{\cdot}001$ (b) $(^-2)^2$ ✶ 4

(c) $(^-0{\cdot}2)^2$ ✶ $0{\cdot}04$ (d) $\frac{1}{9}$ ✶ $\frac{1}{11}$

It can help to show inequations on a number line.
For example:

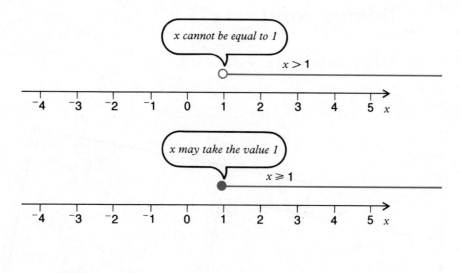

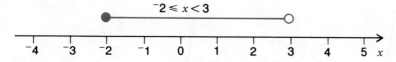

A4 Write down the inequations which fit these lines.

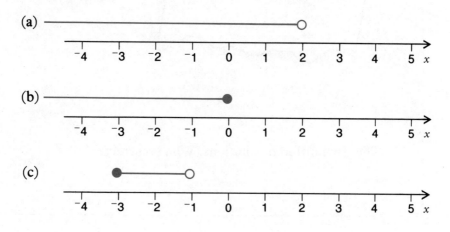

Talking point

Val and Eddie want to solve $^-x < 3$.

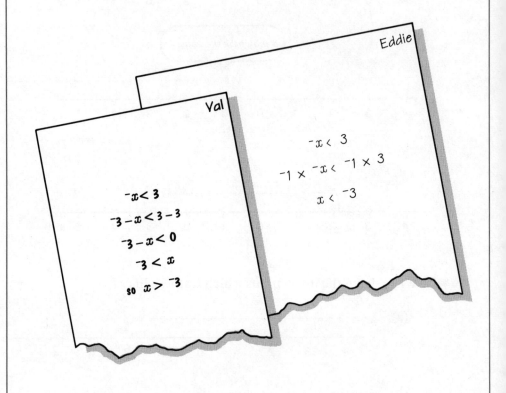

These are different solutions. Who is correct?

A5 What happens to the direction of an inequality if

  (a) the same number is added to each side?

  (b) both sides are multiplied by the same positive number?

  (c) both sides are multiplied by the same negative number?

B Solving inequations

To solve inequations like $3x + 5 \leq 26$ or $4 - 3x < 22$ you proceed as if it were an ordinary equation:

(a)
$$3x + 5 \leq 26$$
$$3x + 5 - 5 \leq 26 - 5 \quad \text{(subtract 5 from both sides)}$$
$$3x \leq 21 \quad \text{(divide both sides by 3)}$$
$$x \leq 7$$

So, for the statement $3x + 5 \leq 26$ to be true, x must have a value of 7 or less.

(b)
$$4 - 3x < 22$$
$$4 - 3x - 4 < 22 - 4 \quad \text{(subtract 4 from both sides)}$$
$$^-3x < 18$$
$$^-x < 6 \quad \text{(divide each side by 3)}$$
$$\text{so } x > ^-6 \quad \text{(look at the Talking point or A5)}$$

B1 Solve these inequations.

(a) $2x + 5 \leq 13$ (b) $3x - 1 \leq 5$ (c) $7 - x > 11$

(d) $5 - 2x > 17$ (e) $\frac{x}{3} + 2 < 5$ (f) $2(x - 1) \leq 12$

(g) $\frac{2x - 1}{3} \geq 3$ (h) $3x - 1 > x + 4$ (i) $4x - 3 < 2x + 1$

One way of checking an equation is to substitute back.
Can you do the same with inequations?
Discuss this with a neighbour.

B2 The length of any side of a triangle is less than the sum of the lengths of the other two sides. For example,

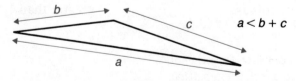

$$a < b + c$$

This diagram shows a triangle and the lengths of its three sides.
Write down three inequations involving these lengths.
Use them to find an inequality for x.

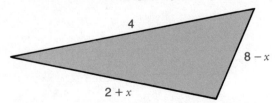

Inequations can be quadratic, for example $x^2 < 16$ or $x^2 + 4x \leq {}^-12$.
Follow this through carefully. Make sure you understand each line.

$$x^2 < 16$$

Think about . . .

$$x^2 = 16$$
$$x^2 - 16 = 0$$
$$(x + 4)(x - 4) = 0$$
$$x + 4 = 0 \text{ or } x - 4 = 0$$

which gives
two separate possible
answers:
$$x = {}^-4 \text{ or } x = 4$$

$$x^2 < 16$$
$$x^2 - 16 < 0$$
$$(x + 4)(x - 4) < 0$$

Here two numbers multiplied
together give an answer less
than zero. The only way this
can be true is for one of them
to be positive, the other negative.
The two possibilities are:

1 $(x + 4) > 0$ and $(x - 4) < 0$
in which case $x > {}^-4$ and $x < 4$

and **2** $(x + 4) < 0$ and $(x - 4) > 0$
in which case $x < {}^-4$ and $x > 4$

Both sets of possible solutions for the inequation can be
shown on a number line like this:

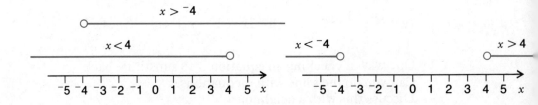

Solution (**1**) is the only possible one.
x must lie between ${}^-4$ and 4.
We can write this as:
${}^-4 < x < 4$

Substitute back into the original
inequation to check this solution.

Solution (**2**) is not possible because x
cannot be both less than ${}^-4$ **and**
greater than 4.

Here is another example, make sure you can follow the working.

$$x^2 + 4x > 12$$
$$x^2 + 4x - 12 > 0$$
$$(x + 6)(x - 2) > 0$$

For this to be true either both $(x + 6)$ and $(x - 2)$ must be positive or both of them must be negative.
Taking each possibility in turn:

1 $x + 6 > 0$ and $x - 2 > 0$ gives $x > {}^-6$ and $x > 2$
Showing these on a number line gives:

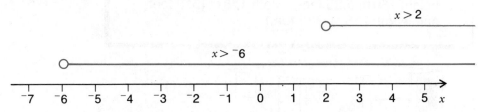

To fit both conditions x must be greater than 2.
So one solution is $x > 2$.

2 $x + 6 < 0$ and $x - 2 < 0$ gives $x < {}^-6$ and $x < 2$
Showing these in a number lines gives –

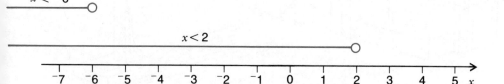

To fit both conditions x must be less than $^-6$.
So another solution is $x < {}^-6$.

The inequation has two solutions: $x > 2$ and $x < {}^-6$

Check these by substituting back into the original inequation.

B3 Solve these inequalities. Check your answers by substituting back.

(a) $x^2 > 9$

(b) $(x + 5)(x - 1) > 0$

(c) $x^2 - 5x < {}^-6$

(d) $x^2 \geq 4$

(e) $x^2 - 6x + 9 > 0$

(f) $2x^2 - 5x < -3$

11 Length, breadth and height

A Cuboids

The largest scientific building in the world is
the vehicle Assembly Building (VAB) at the
Kennedy Space Center. Its dimensions are:
height 160 m (525 feet), width 158 m (518 feet)
and length 218 m (716 feet).

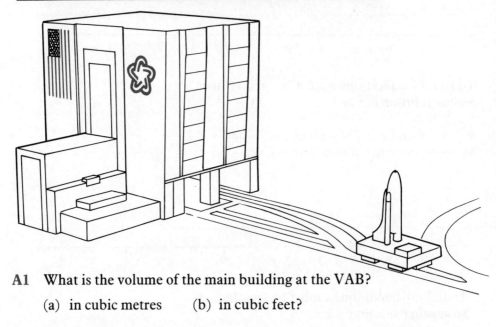

A1   What is the volume of the main building at the VAB?

(a) in cubic metres   (b) in cubic feet?

A2   What is the ground area of the VAB in square metres and square feet?

To find the volume of the VAB – in any units – you need to multiply
together the height, width and length.
These are all lengths. Even if you were working in miles you would still
need to multiply together three lengths.

A3   What is the volume of the VAB in cubic miles?

Calculation of volume will always involve three lengths multiplied together:
(length) × (length) × (length).

We say that the **dimension** of volume is 'length cubed'. This can sometimes
be written as $[L^3]$.

A4 What is the volume of this cuboid?

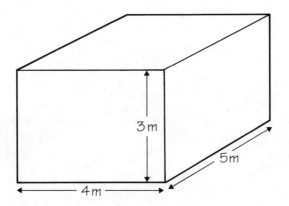

A5 This sketch shows a cuboid.

(a) What is its volume?

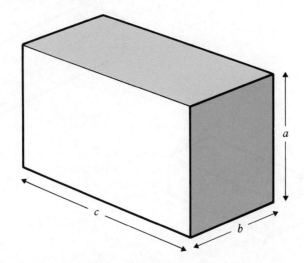

(b) What would be the total volume of five of these cuboids?

(c) What are the **dimensions** of your answers to (a) and (b)?

A6 Write down an expression for the area of this rectangle.

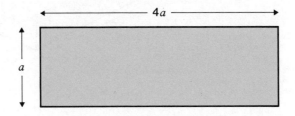

A7 These sketches show several different cuboids, joined together to make a 'U'.

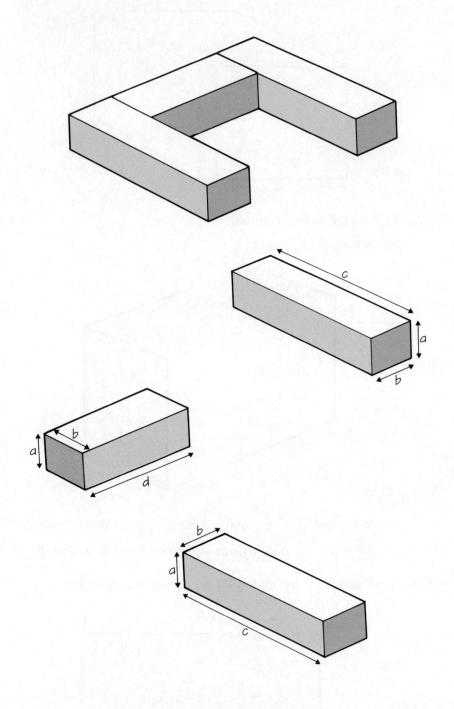

(a) Write down an expression for the volume of the 'U'.

(b) What are the dimensions to your answer in (a)?

The dimension of area is length squared. Whatever units you use, any expression which gives an area must have the dimension of length squared.

A8 Here is part of Tony's homework:

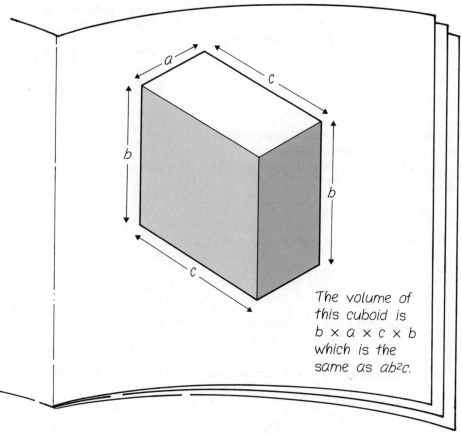

The volume of this cuboid is $b \times a \times c \times b$ which is the same as ab^2c.

(a) How can you tell straight away that his answer is wrong, just by looking at it?

(b) Which of these expressions could not possibly give the surface area of a cuboid?

   (i) $2bc + 2ab + 2ac$

   (ii) $2abc + 2bca$

   (iii) $2abcd$

B Volumes, areas and π

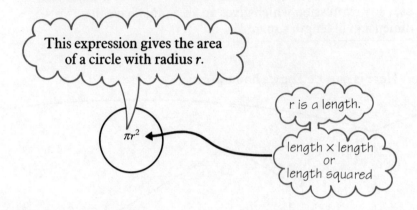

π is a number. It does not have dimensions.
In other words π is **dimensionless**.
It sometimes helps to write an expression like πr^2 in terms
of its dimensions like this:

[number] × [length²]

B1 Another way to look at π is $\pi = \dfrac{\text{circumference}}{2 \times \text{radius}}$

$= \dfrac{\text{circumference}}{\text{diameter}}$

How could you use these to convince someone that π has no
dimensions and is just a number?

B2 Try to work out what the dimensions of the sine of an angle might be.

B3 Just by looking, which of these could not possibly be an expression
for the surface area of a sphere of radius r?

Give reasons for your answers.

(a) $12r^2$ (b) πr^3 (c) $4\pi r^3$

(d) $4\pi r^2$ (e) $4\pi r$ (f) $\dfrac{88r^2}{7}$

Talking point

Safiq is working out the volume of some cylinders.
All the cylinders are 10 cm high.
He wants to investigate how the volume changes
with the radius of the cylinder. Here is some of his working.

I know the formula for the volume of a cylinder.

It is $V = \pi r^2 h$.
r stands for the radius of the cylinder
and h for the height.

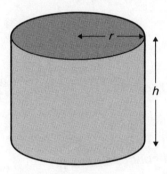

All my cylinders are 10 cm high,
so h is 10 cm. I can use the formula
$10 \pi r^2$ which is easier to use.

The only trouble is, when I checked the dimensions
they turned out to be (number) × (length)^2.

But the dimensions of volume are (length)^3 !!!!!

Where has Safiq gone wrong?

B4 Here are some expressions. The letters a, b, c and h represent lengths.
Some of them give areas, others volumes. Decide which give which.

(a) $\dfrac{4\pi a^2}{3}$ (b) $\pi a^2 + \pi b^2$ (c) πa^2

(d) $(a + b)^2$ (e) $\dfrac{h^2(a + b)}{2}$ (f) $\dfrac{ah}{2}$ (g) $6abc$

B5 Some of these may not be mathematically (or dimensionally) correct. Which ones are they and why? Discuss them together. Explain why they might be used.

(a) Carpet underlay 95p a metre.

(b) A yard of ale.

(c) A light-year is a measure of distance.

(d) Each year hundreds of miles of rain forest are burnt down.

(e) There's about an inch of milk still left in the bottle.

(f) The garden path needs patching up. I'll need about a metre of concrete to fix it.

(g) This can of orange juice holds about 5 fluid ounces.

(h) "But even a litre bottle, big though it is, doesn't get anywhere near to the world's largest bottle which weighed in at 6 feet tall!"

You might find some more like these in newspapers etc.

c True or false?

Looking at dimensions can help jog your memory. Remember π and numbers are dimensionless so it may not always be possible to write down the complete formula.

C1 (a) Look carefully at these clues. Use them to construct the formula for the volume of a cone.

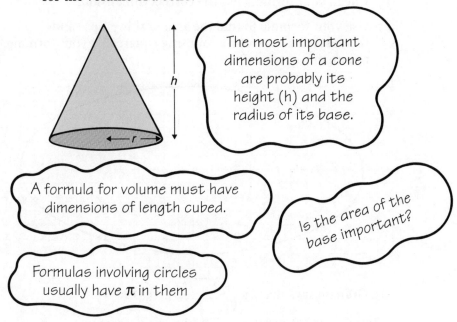

The most important dimensions of a cone are probably its height (h) and the radius of its base.

A formula for volume must have dimensions of length cubed.

Is the area of the base important?

Formulas involving circles usually have π in them

Check your answer with the correct formula.

(b) Try to construct the formula for the surface area of a cone.

C2 Tracey found this formula in a maths book.

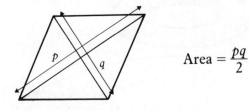

$$\text{Area} = \frac{pq}{2}$$

'The area of a rhombus is half the product of its two diagonals.'

(a) Does the formula work?

(b) Is it dimensionally correct?

C3 (a) Try to construct a formula for the area of an ellipse.

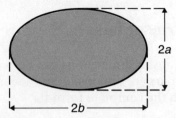

The two most obvious dimensions are a and b ($2a$ and $2b$ are shown in the diagram).

Hint. A circle is a special type of ellipse.

(b) Check your formula has the correct dimension.

(c) Use your formula to find the area of this ellipse and then estimate its area by counting squares. Is your formula reasonably accurate?

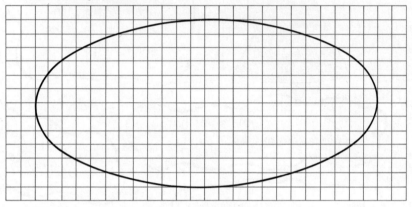

(d) Graham says that $2\pi\sqrt{\dfrac{a^2 + b^2}{2}}$ gives the perimeter of an ellipse. Could he be correct? Discuss this.

C4 A torus is a solid shape similar to a doughnut.

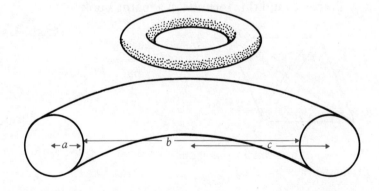

Which of these formula *might* give the volume of a torus?

(a) $\pi a^2 bc$ (b) $4\pi a^2 c$ (c) πabc (d) $\pi(ab)^2$

C5 Which of these – if any – are obviously wrong?
Discuss your reasons.

(a) The area of a circle is half the circumference multiplied by the radius.

(b) The total surface area of a cuboid is $2(ab + bc + ca)$, where a, b and c are the lengths of the sides.

(c)

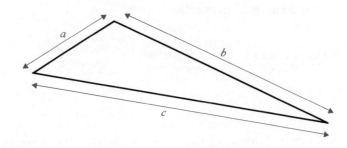

The area of any triangle whose sides are of length a, b and c is

$$\sqrt{s(s-a)(s-b)(s-c)} \text{ where } s = \tfrac{1}{2}(a + b + c)$$

(d)

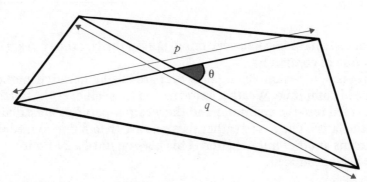

For any quadrilateral having diagonals of length p and q which cut at $\theta°$ the area is $\tfrac{1}{2} pq \sin \theta$.

(e) The regular dodecahedron is a solid with twelve faces.
Each face is a regular pentagon of side a.
A good example of a dodecahedron is a twelve-sided dice.

The surface area of a regular dodecahedron is $3a^2 \sqrt{25 + 10\sqrt{5}}$ and the volume is $\tfrac{1}{4}a^3 (15 + 7\sqrt{5})$.

12 Iteration

A The limit of a sequence

A1 Generate a familiar sequence of numbers by following the instructions in this flowchart.

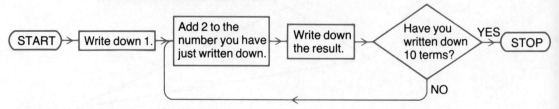

What you have just done is a simple example of an **iterative** process.
Each time you go round the loop, you follow the same set of instructions.

The diagram on the right shows what an
iterative process is.
Each output becomes the input for the
next calculation.

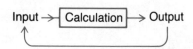

Iterative processes have become very important in the last thirty years, since
the introduction of computers.
Weather forecasts, for example, are now prepared using iterative methods
on a high-speed computer. Weather information from all over the northern
hemisphere is fed into the computer and the weather patterns are calculated
for one minute later. The new weather patterns are then fed in to find the
weather patterns another minute later. This goes on until a 24-hour
forecast has been produced.

The work could be done by people, but by the time they finished, the forecast
would be at least several months out of date!

You can think of the computer as producing a sequence of forecasts in
the same way that you have just produced a sequence of numbers.

The sequence in question A1 is generated by adding 2 to each term to
get the next term.
If we let u_n stand for the nth term of the sequence, and u_{n+1} for
the $(n+1)$th term, the formula for going from u_n to u_{n+1} is

$$u_n + 2 = u_{n+1}.$$

Sometimes we shall call this kind of formula an **iteration formula**.
It will usually be written with the $(n+1)$th term on the left-hand side,
like this:

$$u_{n+1} = u_n + 2.$$

108

A2 The iteration formula of a sequence u is $u_{n+1} = u_n + 5$.
The first term, u_1, is 3.

Write down the values of u_2, u_3, u_4 and u_5.

A3 The iteration formula of a sequence v is $v_{n+1} = 1 \cdot 5 v_n$, and $v_1 = 40$.

Write down the values of v_2, v_3, v_4 and v_5.

A4 Write down the first five terms of the sequence generated by each of these iteration formulas. Start with $u_1 = 9$ each time.

    (a) $u_{n+1} = 2u_n + 1$ (b) $u_{n+1} = \sqrt{u_n}$ (c) $u_{n+1} = 2(u_n + 1)$

A5 A sequence b has the iteration formula $b_{n+1} = \dfrac{b_n}{5} + 4$.

The first term, b_1, is 10. Calculate b_2, b_3, b_4 and b_5.

This iteration was set up on a spreadsheet.

The terms of the sequence get closer and closer to 5 as n increases. We say this sequence **converges** towards 5, and we call 5 the **limit** of the sequence.
All the iterations can be done using a spreadsheet or a programmable calculator.

	A	B
1		10
6		5.0016
7		5.00032
8		5.000064
9		5.0000128

A6 The iteration formula for a sequence c is $c_{n+1} = \dfrac{c_n}{2} + 3$, and $c_1 = 8$.

Calculate the values of c_2, c_3, c_4, . . . and so on, until you are sure what limit the sequence approaches. Write down the limit.

A7 Do the same as in question A6 for the sequence d, where $d_1 = 6$ and the iteration formula is $d_{n+1} = \dfrac{d_n}{4} + 6$.

If we have a sequence which goes 5, $4 \cdot 3$, $4 \cdot 14$, $4 \cdot 021$, $4 \cdot 0081$, . . .
we would decide that its limit appears to be 4.

But suppose we have a sequence which goes like this:
   $1 \cdot 3$, $0 \cdot 94$, $0 \cdot 9247$, $0 \cdot 92324$, $0 \cdot 9232107$, . . .

This sequence does not converge towards an obvious limit.
As the sequence goes on, the first decimal place 'settles down' to a constant value 9, then the second decimal place settles down to 2, and so on.

If we want the limit **correct to 3 decimal places**, it would be $0 \cdot 923$, because after a few terms nothing happens to change the first three places.

A8 A sequence s has the iteration formula $s_{n+1} = \dfrac{1}{s_n} + 5$.

The first term, s_1, is 2.

Calculate the values of $s_2, s_3, s_4, \ldots$ and so on, until you can say what the limit is, correct to 2 decimal places.

B Fixed points

Suppose that the iteration formula of a sequence is $p_{n+1} = \dfrac{p_n}{2} + 2$, and that $p_1 = 8$.

When we calculate p_2, p_3, etc. we get $p_2 = 6$, $p_3 = 5$, $p_4 = 4{\cdot}5$, $p_5 = 4{\cdot}25$.

We can use a set of arrow diagrams to show the sequence being generated.

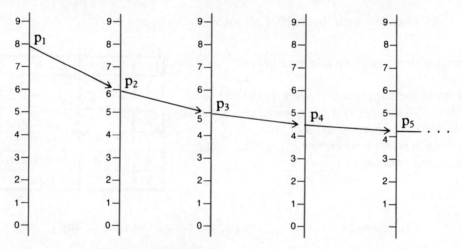

But it is more convenient to use a graph.

Each dot represents a term of the sequence.

The lines joining the dots do not mean anything. They are just there to help the eye.

We shall now investigate what happens when we use the same iteration formula, but different values of p_1.

B1 The graph shows the sequence p, for

which $p_{n+1} = \dfrac{p_n}{2} + 2$, and $p_1 = 8$.

Copy the graph. Show on it also the sequences you get when you use the same iteration formula, but with p_1 equal to (a) 2 (b) 4

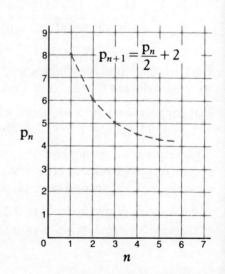

Here is a graph showing the sequences in question **B1**.

The iteration formula is the same for each one:

$$p_{n+1} = \frac{p_n}{2} + 2.$$

The values of p_1 for the three sequences are different.

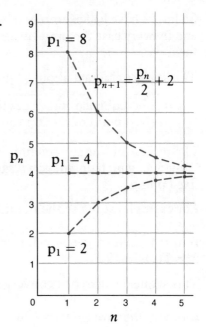

Look at the sequence which starts with $p_1 = 4$.
When p_1 is 4, every term of the sequence is 4.
We say that 4 is a **fixed point** of the iteration

formula $p_{n+1} = \frac{p_n}{2} + 2.$

Look at the sequence which starts with $p_1 = 8$.
The terms of the sequence get closer and closer
to 4 as n increases.
This sequence converges towards 4, which is
the limit of the sequence.

Look at the sequence which starts with $p_1 = 2$.
This sequence also converges towards 4.

B2 The iteration formula for a sequence q is $q_{n+1} = \frac{q_n}{3} + 2.$

  (a) Calculate the first six terms of the sequence q when $q_1 = 12$.

  (b) What number appears to be the limit of the sequence in part (a)?

  (c) Calculate the first six terms of the sequence q when $q_1 = 2$.
    Does this sequence converge to the same limit as before?

  (d) Take the value of the limit in parts (b) and (c) as the value of q_1.
    Calculate the first six terms of the sequence.
    What do you find?

B3 The iteration formula for a sequence r is $r_{n+1} = \frac{r_n + 8}{5}$

  (a) Calculate the first six terms of r when $r_1 = 32$.

  (b) What number appears to be the limit of the sequence?

  (c) Check that the limit is a fixed point of the iteration formula.

B4 The iteration formula for a sequence s is $s_{n+1} = \frac{1}{4}s_n + 12.$

  (a) Choose a value for s_1. Calculate the first six terms of the
    sequence and write down what its limit appears to be.

  (b) Check that the limit is a fixed point of the iteration formula.

So far we have had examples of sequences which converge towards a limit, and in every case the limit turns out to be a fixed point of the iteration formula.

This is a general fact about sequences, which we can state like this:

> If a sequence converges towards a limit, then that limit is a fixed point of the iteration formula for the sequence.

The reverse of this statement is **not** true. There are many examples of sequences which do **not** converge, but whose iteration formulas do have fixed points.

For example, suppose the iteration formula is $u_{n+1} = 2u_n - 3$.

If $u_1 = 4$, then we get $u_2 = 5$, $u_3 = 7$, $u_4 = 11$, $u_5 = 19$,. . .

This sequence does **not** converge.

If $u_1 = 2$, then we get $u_2 = 1$, $u_3 = {}^-1$, $u_4 = {}^-5$, $u_5 = {}^-13$,. . .

This sequence does not converge.

But if $u_1 = 3$, then we get $u_2 = 3$, $u_3 = 3$, $u_4 = 3$, $u_5 = 3$,. . .

So 3 is a fixed point of the iteration formula.

These three sequences are shown in the graph on the right.

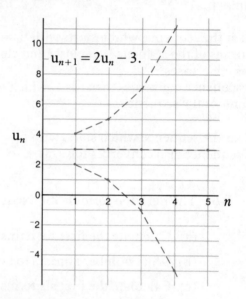

$u_{n+1} = 2u_n - 3.$

B5 The iteration formula of a sequence t is $t_{n+1} = 3t_n - 4$.

    (a) Calculate the first six terms of the sequence when $t_1 = 5$. Does this sequence converge?

    (b) Calculate the first six terms when $t_1 = 1$. Does this sequence converge?

    (c) The formula $t_{n+1} = 3t_n - 4$ does have a fixed point, which is a simple whole number. Find out what it is.

B6 A sequence s has the iteration formula $s_{n+1} = \sqrt{(1 - s_n)}$.
Let $s_1 = 0{\cdot}5$. Calculate the first 10 terms of the sequence.
(If your calculator has a 'change sign' key $\boxed{+/-}$, a good way to do $1 - s_n$ is $s_n \boxed{+/-}\boxed{+}\boxed{1}\boxed{=}$.)

The sequence converges towards a limit whose value to 3 d.p. is $0{\cdot}618$. The terms are alternately above and below the limit. Check that $0{\cdot}618$ is, approximately, a fixed point of the iteration formula.

C Iteration formulas with more than one fixed point

The iteration formula for a sequence v is $v_{n+1} = \dfrac{2}{v_n + 1}$.

When you have to use an iteration formula, it is worth spending a few moments deciding how you can best use your calculator. You want to avoid having to key in long strings of digits.

One way to do $\dfrac{2}{v_n + 1}$ is to use the **reciprocal key** $\boxed{\tfrac{1}{x}}$.

You do $\dfrac{v_n + 1}{2}$ first and then 'invert' it by using $\boxed{\tfrac{1}{x}}$.

One possible key sequence for the formula is given here. (You will have to check that it works on your calculator.)

Enter the value of v_1 $\boxed{+}\,\boxed{1}\,\boxed{=}\,\boxed{\div}\,\boxed{2}\,\boxed{=}\,\boxed{\tfrac{1}{x}}$

C1 Copy the table below (or use a spreadsheet to produce the results). Calculate the first 8 terms of the sequence v whose iteration formula is given above, for the different first terms given in the table.

Enter the results in your table (to 3 d.p.) and describe the behaviour of each sequence.
(This can be done as a group activity, with different people doing different sequences.)

v_1	v_2	v_3	v_4	v_5	v_6	v_7	v_8	Behaviour
3	0·5	1·333	0·857	1·077	0·963	1·019	0·991	Converges towards 1
2								
1								
0								
⁻1								
⁻2								
⁻3								
⁻4								

C2 Try some more values for v_1. See if you can get a sequence which converges towards a limit of ⁻2 (one of the fixed points of the iteration formula.)

C3 The iteration formula $w_{n+1} = w_n^2$ has two fixed points which are both easy to spot. What are they?
Investigate the behaviour of the sequence w when w_1 is
(a) greater than 1   (b) between 0 and 1   (c) less than 0

Back of an envelope 3

1   Here are some more calculations scribbled on the back of an envelope. Make sure you are able to follow the working.

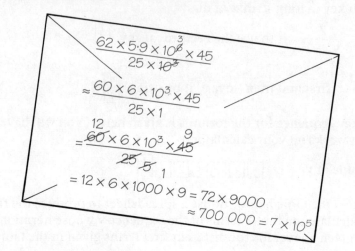

$$\frac{62 \times 5 \cdot 9 \times 10^{\cancel{6}\,3} \times 45}{25 \times \cancel{10^3}}$$

$$\approx \frac{60 \times 6 \times 10^3 \times 45}{25 \times 1}$$

$$= \frac{\overset{12}{\cancel{60}} \times 6 \times 10^3 \times \overset{9}{\cancel{45}}}{\underset{1}{\cancel{25}}\ \cancel{5}}$$

$$= 12 \times 6 \times 1000 \times 9 = 72 \times 9000$$

$$\approx 700\ 000 = 7 \times 10^5$$

Work out the approximate answers to these questions.

(a) $\dfrac{4 \cdot 1 \times 10^4 \times 587}{7 \cdot 8 \times 10^3}$

(b) $\dfrac{4 \cdot 9 \times 10^4 \times 3 \cdot 1}{2 \cdot 0 \times 10^3}$

(c) $\dfrac{1 \cdot 7 \times 10^2 \times 5 \cdot 9}{3 \cdot 9 \times 10^{-1}}$

When you have finished, compare your working and answers with a partner.
See how close you were by using a calculator.

2   Check these calculations by doing approximate calculations.

(a) $\dfrac{21 \cdot 8 \times 10^{-19}}{1 \cdot 6 \times 10^{-19}} = 4 \cdot 83565$

(b) $\dfrac{6 \cdot 6 \times 10^{-34}}{7 \cdot 7 \times 10^{-24}} = 8 \cdot 6 \times 10^{-9}$

3   Bangladesh has a population of 107 million. It has 21 400 hospital beds. Finland has 75 000 hospital beds and a population of 4 986 000.

Complete this table showing the number of hospital beds per 1000 people. (Don't use a calculator – just pencil and paper!)

Country	Population	Number of hospital beds	Number of hospital beds per 1000 people
Bangladesh	107 million	21 400	
Finland	4 986 000	75 000	

4   Calculate each of these as accurately as you think necessary.

(a) In Turkey there are 172 TV sets per 1000 people.
The population of Turkey is 56·1 million.
How many TV sets are there in Turkey?

(b) The area of Mexico is 1958 thousand square kilometres.
It has a population of 86 154 thousand.
How many people is this per square kilometre?

(c) In 1791 Thomas Paine wrote *The Rights of Man*.
It is a book which suggests aid for the poor, education for all and old age pensions. In it Paine tried to estimate the number of people over fifty years old in England.

> I have several times counted the persons I met in the streets of London, men, women and children, and have generally found that the average number (of people fifty or above) is about one in sixteen or seventeen.

Using these figures Paine estimated that four hundred and twenty thousand were aged 50+. What was the population of England at this time? Was Paine's method a good one to use? Why?

(d) A good typist can type about 200 words a minute.
How long would it take to type a million words at this rate?

13 The graphs of the trigonometric functions

A Amplitude and period

The graph of the function $y = \sin x$ has a 'wave' shape. (In fact the graph is often called a 'sine wave'.) The period of the graph is 360°.

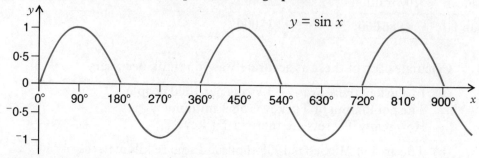

By making slight alterations to the function, we can modify the graph without altering the overall 'wave' shape.

The graph of $y = \sin x$ oscillates between a maximum value of 1 and a minimum value of $^-1$.
1 is called the **amplitude** of the wave.

We can alter the amplitude by multiplying $\sin x$ by a number, for example 1·5. This gives us the function $y = 1·5 \sin x$, whose graph looks like this. The amplitude is 1·5. (The period is still 360°.)

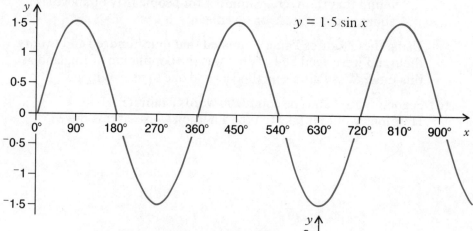

A1 (a) What is the amplitude of the sine wave shown on the right?

(b) Write down the equation in the form $y = \ldots$

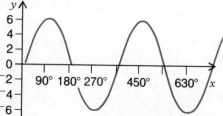

116

Another way to vary the graph is to replace sin x by sin $2x$, sin $3x$, etc.

'sin $2x$' means 'the sine of twice x'.
So if x is, say, 30°, then $2x$ is 60° and sin $2x$ is sin 60°, or **0·866.** . .

A2 Draw axes with x from 0° to 360°.

(a) Calculate the value of sin x when x is 0°, 30°, 60°, 90°, . . . up to 360° and draw the graph of $y = \sin x$.

(b) Copy and complete this table of values for the function $y = \sin 2x$. (Work to 2 d.p.)

x	0°	30°	60°	90°	120°	. . . up to 360°
sin $2x$	0	0·87				

When $x = 30°$, $2x = 60°$. So sin $2x = \sin 60° = 0·87$.

(c) Draw the graph of $y = \sin 2x$ on the same axes as before. You may need to work out sin $2x$ for intermediate values of x.

Similarly the graph of $y = \cos x$ oscillates between a maximum value of 1 and a minimum value of $^-1$.

A3 Draw axes with x from 0° to 360°.

(a) Calculate the value of cos x when x is 0°, 30°, 60°, . . . up to 360° and draw the graph of $y = \cos x$.

(b) Look back at the graph you drew for question **A2** (a).
What is the relationship between the two graphs?

(c) Copy and complete this table of values for $y = \cos 2x$. (Work to 2 d.p.)

x	0°	30°	60°	. . . . up to 360°
y	1	0·5	. . .	

(d) Draw the graph of $y = \cos 2x$ on the same axes as before.
You may need to work out cos $2x$ for some intermediate values of x.
What is the period of the graph?

We can work out the period of the functions $y = \sin 2x$ or $y = \cos 2x$ without actually drawing the graphs.

The graphs of $y = \sin x$ and $y = \cos x$ repeat after 360°.

So the graphs of $y = \sin 2x$ and $y = \cos 2x$ will repeat when $2x$ reaches 360°.
In other words they will repeat when x reaches 180°, so their period is 180°.

We can alter the amplitude by multiplying $2x$ by a number.
Here, for example, is the graph of $y = 4 \sin 2x$, with amplitude 4.

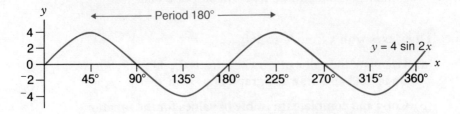

A4   (a) The graph of $y = \sin 3x$ will repeat itself when $3x$ reaches $360°$.
What is the period of the graph of $y = \sin 3x$?

(b) What is the amplitude of the graph of $y = 4 \sin 3x$?

A5   Write down the amplitude and the period of the graph of
each of these functions.

(a) $y = 5 \sin 2x$ (b) $y = 10 \sin 3x$ (c) $y = 20 \sin (\frac{1}{2}x)$
(d) $y = 8 \sin 3x$ (e) $y = 6 \cos 4x$

Investigate what happens for graphs of $y = a \tan bx$ for different
values of a and b. Write a short report about your findings.

B   Applications

This table shows the length of day (sunrise to sunset) in Newcastle,
every ten days during a typical year.

Date	n(day number)	L(length in hours)	Date	n(day number)	L(length in hours)
10 Jan	10	7·6	9 July	190	17·1
20 Jan	20	8·0	19 July	200	16·7
30 Jan	30	8·6	29 July	210	16·1
9 Feb	40	9·3	8 Aug	220	15·5
19 Feb	50	10·0	18 Aug	230	14·8
1 Mar	60	10·7	28 Aug	240	14·1
11 Mar	70	11·5	7 Sept	250	13·4
21 Mar	80	12·2	17 Sept	260	12·7
31 Mar	90	12·9	27 Sept	270	11·9
10 Apr	100	13·7	7 Oct	280	11·2
20 Apr	110	14·4	17 Oct	290	10·5
30 Apr	120	15·1	27 Oct	300	9·7
10 May	130	15·8	6 Nov	310	9·1
20 May	140	16·4	16 Nov	320	8·4
30 May	150	16·9	26 Nov	330	7·9
9 June	160	17·2	6 Dec	340	7·5
19 June	170	17·4	16 Dec	350	7·2
29 June	180	17·3	26 Dec	360	7·3

B1 The graph below was drawn from the information in the table.
A school in Newcastle plans a sponsored walk on 15 April. Estimate
the length of the day on 15 April, using either the graph or the table.

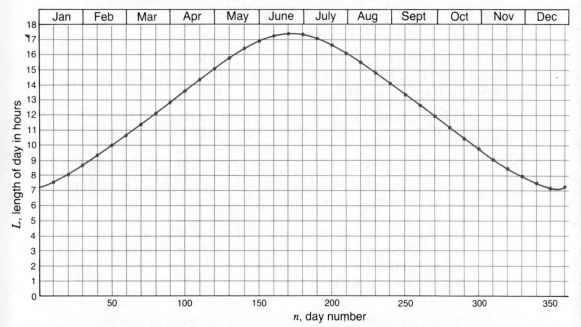

B2 Estimate each of these.
  (a) Which is the longest day? (Estimate its date.)
  (b) Which is the shortest day?
  (c) When is the day 12 hours long? (Estimate the dates.)

B3 (a) How much longer is the day on 9 February than on 30 January?
  (b) How much longer is the day on 30 April than on 20 April?
  (c) In what part of the year are the days lengthening fastest?
  (d) When are they shortening fastest?

The graph looks similar in shape to a sine curve, but it does not
drop below the horizontal axis.

In fact there is a formula with a sine in it which fits the curve
quite well. It is
  $L = 12 \cdot 3 + 5 \sin (0 \cdot 986n - 80 \cdot 8)$

n stands for the number of the day, and L for the length of that day
in hours (in Newcastle).

B4 The formula is only approximately true. It is less accurate
than the table. Use the formula to find the length of day on
these dates, and compare your result with the table.

  (a) 9 February (n is 40. Start by calculating $0 \cdot 986n - 80 \cdot 8$,
     find the sine of this, multiply by 5 and then add $12 \cdot 3$.)

  (b) 31 March (c) 8 August (d) 6 December

119

The length of day on any given date depends on the **latitude** of the place where you are.
If you know the length of day in Newcastle, you can find the length of day in other places in the British Isles by using this formula:

$$L' = (0{\cdot}04\lambda - 1{\cdot}2)L + 26{\cdot}4 - 0{\cdot}48\lambda$$

L' stands for the length of day at the place you are interested in.
λ (the Greek letter l, called 'lambda') stands for the latitude of the place.
L stands for the length of day in Newcastle.

This formula too is only approximately true. It is reasonably accurate for latitudes between 50°N and 60°N. Outside this range it is inaccurate.

B5 (a) Use the table to find the length of day in Newcastle on 16 November.
(b) Use the formula for L' to find the length of day in Bristol on 16 November. The latitude of Bristol is 51·5°N.

B6 Use the first formula on this page to find the length of day in Newcastle on your birthday. Estimate from an atlas the latitude of your home (to the nearest 0·1°) and use the second formula to find the length of day at home on your birthday.

B7 Here is an equilateral triangle of side 2 units and an isosceles triangle whose hypotenuse is 2 units. Check that you agree with the other lengths.

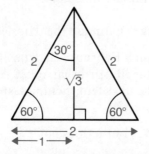 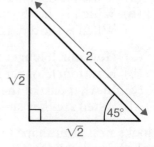

Use the triangles to help you complete this table for sin x. Write the answers in the same form as those for cos x. The first one has been done for you.

$x°$	0	30	45	60	90	120	135	150	180
cos x	$\dfrac{\sqrt{4}}{2}$	$\dfrac{\sqrt{3}}{2}$	$\dfrac{\sqrt{2}}{2}$	$\dfrac{\sqrt{1}}{2}$	$\dfrac{\sqrt{0}}{2}$	$\dfrac{^-\sqrt{1}}{2}$	$\dfrac{^-\sqrt{2}}{2}$	$\dfrac{^-\sqrt{3}}{2}$	$\dfrac{^-\sqrt{4}}{2}$
sin x	$\dfrac{\sqrt{0}}{2}$								

Extend the table – does the pattern still hold?
Do values of tan x follow a similar pattern?

120

14 Inequalities

A Regions

When we use x- and y-coordinates to
describe the positions of points in a
plane, then **lines** can be described by
equations.

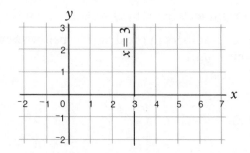

The line shown in the diagram has
the equation $x = 3$.

The line $x = 3$ is the boundary between two **regions**, one either side
of the line.
Every point in the left-hand region has an x-coordinate which is
less than 3. Every point in the right-hand region has an x-coordinate
which is greater than 3.

We can describe the two regions by
inequalities.

To the left of the line is the region $x < 3$.

To the right of the line is the region $x > 3$.

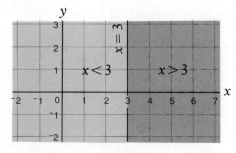

A1 Write down an inequality which describes each **unshaded** region.

(a)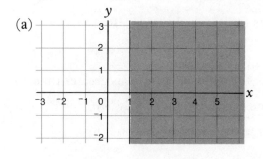

(b)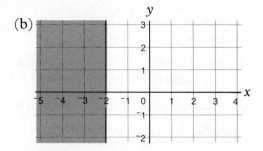

(c)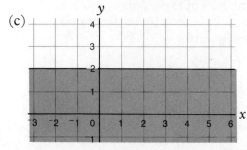

(d)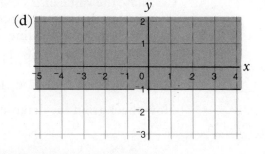

Think about the expression $2x + 3y$.
If you say what the values of x and y are to be, then the value
of $2x + 3y$ can be calculated.
So what we have is a **function** of x and y, which we can write as

$(x, y) \rightarrow 2x + 3y$.

For example, when $(x, y) = (4, 1)$, then $2x + 3y = 8 + 3 = 11$.

The red numbers in the diagram below show the value of $2x + 3y$ at
various points.

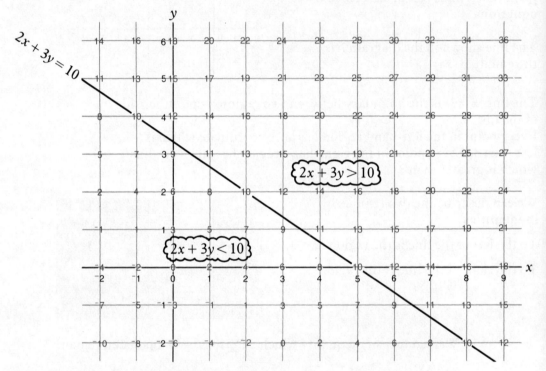

The sloping line goes through all the points for which $2x + 3y = 10$, so its
equation is $2x + 3y = 10$.

The line $2x + 3y = 10$ separates the plane into two regions.
At every point in the region **above** the line, the value of $2x + 3y$ is greater than 10.

So we can describe the region above the line as the region $2x + 3y > 10$.

Similarly, the region below the line is the region $2x + 3y < 10$.

A2   Calculate the value of $2x + 3y$ at each of these points and
say whether they are in the region $2x + 3y > 10$ or the region
$2x + 3y < 10$, or on the line $2x + 3y = 10$.

(a) $(4·5, 0·5)$ (b) $(3·5, 1)$ (c) $(9·5, {}^-2·5)$

(d) $({}^-3·5, 5·5)$ (e) $(2·6, 1·5)$

Now check from the diagram where possible.

It is not always true that the inequality with '>' describes the region above a line, and the inequality with '<' the region below the line.

The red numbers on this diagram show the value of $x - y$ at various points.

For example, at the point $(3, 2)$ the value of $x - y = 3 - 2 = 1$.

The sloping line has the equation $x - y = 3$.

You can see from the diagram that at every point **above** the line, $x - y$ is less than 3, and at every point **below** the line, $x - y$ is greater than 3.

So **above** the line is the region $x - y < 3$, and **below** the line is the region $x - y > 3$.

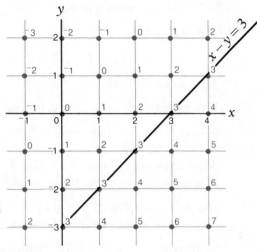

Suppose that all you are given is the line $x - y = 3$. You do not know which side of the line is the region $x - y < 3$, and which side is $x - y > 3$.

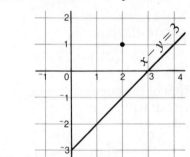

All you need to do is to test **one** point which is not on the line itself.

For example, take the point $(2, 1)$, which is **above** the line.

Does $(2, 1)$ satisfy $x - y < 3$ or $x - y > 3$?

It satisfies $x - y < 3$, because $2 - 1 = 1$, which is less than 3.

So above the line is the region $x - y < 3$, (and below is $x - y > 3$).

A3 Write down an inequality which describes each **unshaded** region. (Use the 'test point' method described above.)

(a)

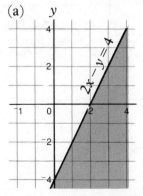

(b)

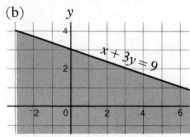

(c)

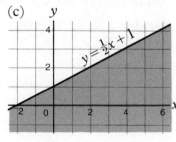

Drawing regions

We show a region in a drawing by shading out the part of the plane which does **not** belong to it.

Worked example

Draw the region $3x + 4y > 18$.

First draw the line $3x + 4y = 18$.

The easiest way to do this is to find where the line crosses the axes.

When $x = 0$, $4y = 18$, so $y = 4\frac{1}{2}$.   When $y = 0$, $3x = 18$, so $x = 6$.

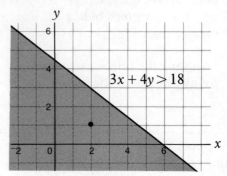

After drawing the line $3x + 4y = 18$, choose a 'test point' not on it, for example $(2, 1)$.

At $(2, 1)$ the value of $3x + 4y$ is $6 + 4 = 10$. So $(2, 1)$ is in the region $3x + 4y < 18$.

So the region $3x + 4y > 18$ is **above** the line.

So shade out the part of the plane **below** the line.

A4   Draw the region $2x + y < 6$.

A5   Draw each of the following regions on separate diagrams.

    (a) $2x - y > 5$ (b) $x - 3y < 6$ (c) $x - y > {}^-3$ (d) $y < 2x$

A region may have a curve as a boundary. If the equation of the curve is in the form '$y = $ a function of x', then it is easy to write down inequalities for the regions above and below the curve.

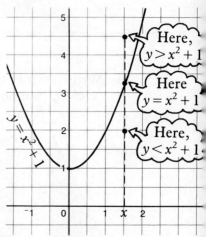

For example, this diagram shows the curve whose equation is $y = x^2 + 1$.

For any given value of x, the point where $y = x^2 + 1$ lies on the curve. At points above the curve, the value of y will be greater than $x^2 + 1$, and at points below the curve, y will be less than $x^2 + 1$.

So **above** the curve is the region $y > x^2 + 1$.

And **below** the curve is the region $y < x^2 + 1$.

(The same idea also works for a straight line, when its equation is in the form '$y = \ldots$').

A6   Draw the graph of $y = x(4 - x)$ for values of x from ${}^-1$ to 5. On the diagram show the region $y < x(4 - x)$.

B Regions with two boundaries

The region above line a is the region $x+y>4$.

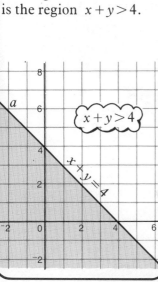

The region below line b is the region $y<2x$.

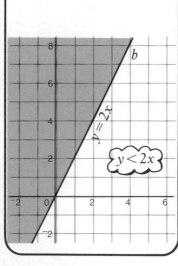

The region which is both above line a and below b is described by the two inequalities together.

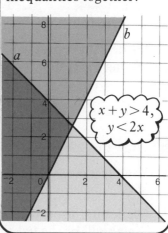

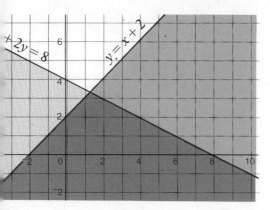

B1 Choose a test point somewhere inside the unshaded region in the diagram on the left.

(a) Does your test point satisfy
$x+2y<8$ **or** $x+2y>8$?

(b) Does your test point satisfy
$y<x+2$ **or** $y>x+2$?

(c) Write down the pair of inequalities which describe the unshaded region.

B2 Write down a pair of inequalities which describes each unshaded region.

(a)

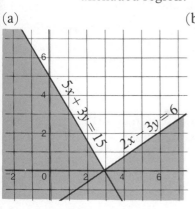

(b)

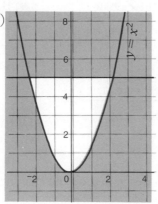

(c)

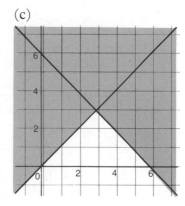

125

Worked example

Draw the region described by the inequalities $x - 2y > 4$, $x + 3y > 6$.

1 Draw the line $x - 2y = 4$.

Use a test point to decide which side of the line is $x - 2y < 4$ and which is $x - 2y > 4$.

Shade out the part you do not want, leaving the region $x - 2y > 4$.

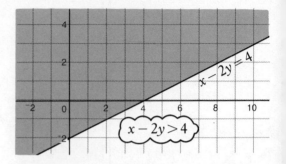

2 Draw the line $x + 3y = 6$.

Use a test point to decide which side of the line is which.

Shade out the part you do not want. (Some will be shaded already.)

The region left unshaded satisfies both inequalities $x - 2y > 4$ and $x + 3y > 6$.

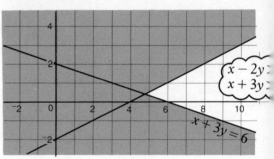

B3 Draw the region described by the two inequalities $x + y < 5$ and $y > x$.

B4 Draw the region described by the two inequalities $x + 2y > 8$ and $y < 5$.

B5 Draw the region described by the two inequalities $x - y < 3$ and $2x + 3y < 12$.

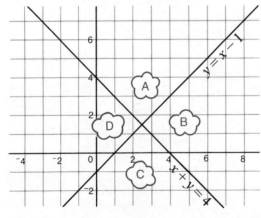

B6 The two lines $x + y = 4$ and $y = x - 1$ divide the plane into four regions A, B, C and D.

Write down the pair of inequalities which describes each of the four regions A, B, C and D.

B7 Draw the region described by the two inequalities $y > x^2$ and $y < 2x$.

B8 Draw the region described by the two inequalities $y > x(x - 2)$ and $y < x(4 - x)$.

126

10 Inequations

10.1 If $a = 2$, $b = {}^-2$ and $c = 1$ write down as many inequalities as you can involving a, b and c, no more than once each. Here is one to start off with $ab < c$.

10.2 Solve these inequations.

(a) $2x < 10$ (b) $2x \geq 10$ (c) $x + 3 < 10$ (d) $4 < {}^-x$

(e) $4(x - 1) \geq 2x$ (f) $10 - x < 5$ (g) $x - 7 > 4x + 5$

10.3 Solve these inequalities. Check your answers by substituting back.

(a) $x^2 < 1$ (b) $x^2 \geq 1$ (c) $x^2 + 5x \geq {}^-6$

10.4 Write down the inequalities which fit these lines.

(a)
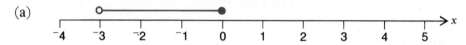

(b)
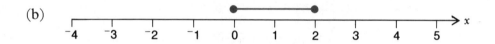

(c)
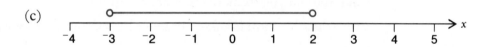

10.5 Find the whole number solutions to each of these inequations

(a) $0 \leq x \leq 2$ (b) ${}^-2 < x \leq 0$ (c) $6 \leq 2x \leq 8$ (d) $0 \leq x^2 \leq 4$

11 Length, breadth and height

11.1 A rectangle's sides have lengths x and y and diagonal length z. Which of these could not possibly be the formula for its area?

(a) xyz (b) $x\sqrt{z^2 - x^2}$ (c) $y\sqrt{z^2 - y^2}$

11.2 Which of these are obviously incorrect?

(a)

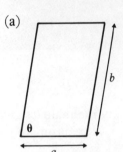

The area of this
parallelogram
is $ab\sin\theta$.

(b) Another formula
for the area is
$a(\sin\theta)^2$

(c) A rhombus whose
diagonals are of
length e and f has an
area of $\frac{1}{2}ef$.

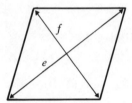

(d) The area of a triangle whose sides are lengths a, b and c
is $\sqrt{s(s-a)(s-b)(s-c)}$ where $s = (a+b+c)\div 2$.

(e) The volume of a cube of side a is $6a^2$.

(f) The formula of a sphere of radius r is $4\pi r^2$.

12 Iteration

12.1 The iteration formula of a sequence s is $s_{n+1} = \dfrac{s_n + 1}{5}$.

(a) Start with $s_1 = 0$ and calculate s_2, s_3, . . . up to s_8.

(b) What limit do you think the sequence converges towards?

(c) Check that this limit is a fixed point of the iteration formula.

12.2 The iteration formula for a sequence u is $u_{n+1} = \sqrt{(u_n + 1)}$.

(a) Start with $u_1 = 0$ and calculate u_2, u_3, . . . until the second
decimal place no longer changes.

(b) Write down the limit of the sequence to 2 decimal places.

13 The graphs of the trigonometric functions

13.1 The graph on the right
is the graph of one of
these functions. Which
one is it?

$y = \sin 2x \qquad y = \sin\dfrac{x}{2}$

$y = 2\sin x \qquad y = \frac{1}{2}\sin x$

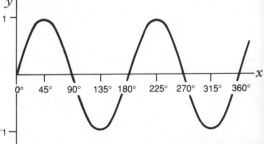

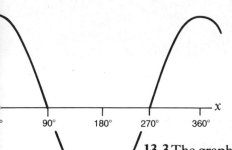

13.2 The graph on the left is the graph of one of these four functions. Which function is it?

$$y = \sin 2x \quad y = 2 \sin x$$
$$y = \cos 2x \quad y = 2 \cos x$$

13.3 The graph on the right is the graph of one of these equations. Which equation is it?

$y = \tan \frac{1}{2}x$
$y = \tan x$
$y = \tan 2x$
$y = \tan 4x$

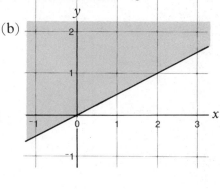

Inequalities

14.1 Draw axes with values of x and y from $^-5$ to 5.
Draw the line whose equation is $2x - 3y = 6$.
Show the region $2x - 3y > 6$ by shading out the unwanted part.

14.2 Write down inequalities which describe the unshaded regions below.

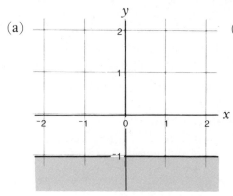

14.3 Write down a pair of inequalities which describes the unshaded region here.

(You may find it useful to choose a 'test point' somewhere in the region.)

14.4 Draw axes with x and y from $^-3$ to 3. Indicate clearly the region described by the two inequalities $y > x$ and $y < 2 - x^2$.

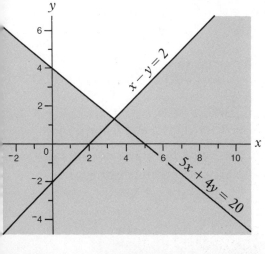

1 Whole numbers and decimals

1.1 Without using a calculator, say which of these you could buy with a £20 note.
  (a) 38 metres of hosepipe at 47p per metre
  (b) 4·5 metres of curtain fabric at £5·25 per metre
  (c) 120 metres of nylon rope at 21p per metre

1.2 When Brenda puts her gas fire on 'high', the gas it uses costs 68p per hour. How much does it cost to have it on
  (a) for 8 hours   (b) for $2\frac{1}{4}$ hours
  (c) over the weekend, from 6 p.m. Friday to 8 a.m. Monday

1.3 (a) 6 people share a 5 kg sack of potatoes. What weight does each get?
  (b) 5 people share a 6 kg sack. What weight does each get?

1.4 A station buffet sells coffee in standard cups (240 ml) at 38p, or in large beakers (330 ml) at 55p. Which is better value?

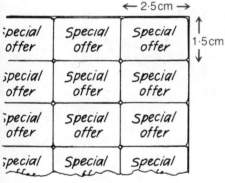

1.5 This picture shows a sheet of stick-on labels. Each label is 2·5 cm wide and 1·5 cm high. The sheet is 65 cm wide and 48 cm high.

How many labels are there on the sheet?

1.6 A bottle contains 0·6 litre of cough mixture. The 'adult dose' is three medicine spoonfuls. A medicine spoon holds 5 ml.

How many adult doses can you get from the bottle

1.7 Round off (a) 37·886 to 2 d.p.   (b) 37·886 to 2 s.f.
  (c) 0·039 862 to 3 s.f.   (d) 362 598 to 3 s.f.

1.8 Write these numbers in standard index form.
  (a) 20 000 000   (b) 0·000 08   (c) 3 620 000   (d) 0·000 009 27

1.9 The value of a is known to be somewhere between 2·4 and 2·5. The value of b is known to be somewhere between 4·8 and 5·0.

  (a) Calculate the minimum and maximum possible values of ab.

  (b) Calculate the minimum and maximum possible values of $\frac{a}{b}$.

1.10 A racing car was timed over a measured distance. The distance was 500·0 metres, correct to the nearest 0·1 m. The time taken was 4·58 seconds, correct to the nearest 0·01 second.

(a) State the minimum and maximum possible values for the actual distance travelled by the car.

(b) Do the same for the actual time taken.

(c) Calculate, to 2 d.p., maximum and minimum values for the average speed of the car, in m/s.

2 Percentage

2.1 Calculate   (a) 45% of £280   (b) 8% of £17·50

	Male	Female
Under 18	23	19
18 or over	63	70

2.2 This table gives some information about 175 people living in a block of flats.

(a) What percentage of the 175 people are males aged 18 or over?

(b) What percentage are females under 18?

(c) What percentage **of the males** are under 18?

(d) What percentage of the under-18s are male?

2.3 (a) Alice's salary is £8260. It goes up by 15%. What is it after the increase?

(b) Ada's salary goes up from £7230 to £8240. What is the percentage increase?

2.4 Calculate the percentage reduction in each of these, to the nearest 1%.

(a) A car salesman reduces the price of a car from £3000 to £2750.

(b) An estate agent reduces the price of a house from £49 500 to £47 500.

(c) A dress shop reduces the price of a £75 dress by £20.

2.5 (a) Between January 1986 and January 1987, the average price of a house on Meadowside went up by 7%. What is the multiplier from the January 1986 price to the January 1987 price?

Jan 1986 price ——| ×? ⟩—→ Jan 1987 price

(b) Between January 1987 and January 1988, the average price went up by 12%. Calculate the overall percentage increase between January 1986 and January 1988.

2.6 In March a camera shop raised the price of a camera by 16%. In September they had a sale, in which all prices were reduced by 15%.

Was the sale price higher or lower than the price before March? Give the reason for your answer.

2.7 A newspaper reporting a flu epidemic in a village said that women had been worse affected than men. It stated that out of 450 cases of flu, 271 were women and 179 men.

	Caught flu	Did not catch flu
Men	179	88
Women	271	159

The actual data on which the paper based its conclusion is shown in this table. Do you agree with the paper's conclusion? If not, state your reasons clearly.

3 Fractions

3.1 The sizes of five nuts (in inches) are $\frac{11''}{16}$, $\frac{1''}{2}$, $\frac{5''}{8}$, $\frac{15''}{16}$ and $\frac{3''}{4}$. Put them in order of size, starting with the smallest.

3.2 You are trying to tighten a bolt. A $\frac{3''}{4}$ spanner is just too small. A $\frac{7''}{8}$ spanner is just too big. Which size is halfway between the two?

3.3 1 inch is equal to 25·4 mm.
What are these equal to in mm, to the nearest 0·1 mm?
(a) $\frac{1''}{4}$ (b) $\frac{3''}{4}$ (c) $\frac{5''}{8}$ (d) $\frac{13''}{16}$

3.4 On a rabbit farm, $\frac{2}{5}$ of the rabbits are male, and $\frac{3}{4}$ of the male rabbits are white. What fraction of all the rabbits are white males?

4 Ratio

4.1 The 'aspect ratio' of a cinema screen is the ratio $\dfrac{\text{width}}{\text{height}}$.

(a) Calculate the aspect ratio of each of these screens, to 2 d.p.

A: 5·7 m wide, 4·3 m high   B: 10·6 m wide, 5·2 m high
C: 7·8 m wide, 5·2 m high   D: 7·2 m wide, 4·8 m high

(b) Which of the four screens are similar to each other?

4.2 Calculate these multipliers, to 3 significant figures.

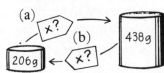
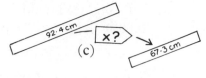

4.3 In an equilateral triangle, the ratio $\dfrac{\text{height}}{\text{base}}$ is 0·866 (to 3 s.f.).

Use this fact to calculate
(a) the height of an equilateral triangle whose base is 4·5 cm
(b) the base of an equilateral triangle whose height is 7·2 cm

4.4 A grocer mixes good quality and poor quality tea in the ratio 3 to 5 by weight. What percentage of the mixture is good quality tea?

5 Gradient

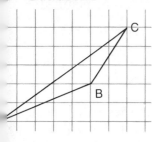

5.1 Calculate the gradient of   (a) AB   (b) BC   (c) AC

5.2 These are rough sketches of two hills, P and Q.
Which hill is steeper, and why?

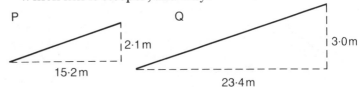

5.3 Calculate the gradient of the line joining
(a) $(0, 0)$ and $(4, {}^-2)$ (b) $({}^-1, 4)$ and $(4, 5)$ (c) $({}^-2, 5)$ and $(6, {}^-1)$

6 Rates

6.1 (a) A tap takes 12·5 minutes to fill a 60-litre water tank.
Calculate the rate of flow of the tap in litre/min.
(b) How long would it take to fill the same tank from a tap
which flows at 18·5 litre/min?

6.2 An oven is turned on. The temperature rises slowly at first, then
faster, and then more slowly again until it reaches a maximum.
Then it stays constant. Sketch a graph to show all this.

6.3 Worldwings Airways use AX7 aircraft on their flights from London
to Moscow, a distance of 1880 miles. The flight takes $4\frac{1}{4}$ hours.
(a) Calculate the average speed of the aircraft.
(b) The airline considers replacing the AX7 by another plane,
which can fly at an average speed of 530 m.p.h. If they
do this, what will the new flight time be?

6.4 This table shows distances and times for a train journey.

Distance from London (miles):	0		209	299		401
	London		Preston	Carlisle		Glasgow
Time:	12:45		15:30	16:45		18:15

(a) Calculate the average speed of the train between
(i) London and Preston   (ii) Preston and Carlisle
(iii) Carlisle and Glasgow
(b) Calculate the overall average speed for the whole journey, to 1 d.p.

6.5 A solution of copper sulphate contains 0·85 g of copper sulphate per litre.
(a) How much copper sulphate is there in 0·35 litre of solution?
(b) What volume of the solution contains 0·50 g of copper sulphate?

133

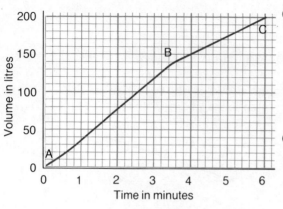

Volume in litres (y-axis): 0, 50, 100, 150, 200
Time in minutes (x-axis): 0, 1, 2, 3, 4, 5, 6

6.6 This graph shows the amount of liquic in a tank while it was being filled.

Calculate the average rate at which the water entered the tank
(a) between A and B
(b) between B and C

6.7 Pat is crossing the desert in a truck. She starts with a full fuel tank holding 140 litres of fuel. After travelling 80 m she has used up 25 litres.

She still has 390 miles to go. Will she make it?

7 Constructing formulas

7.1 These arrangements are made with red and black balls joined together.

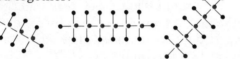

(a) How many black balls will there be when there are 20 red balls?

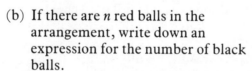

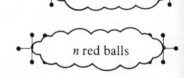

20 red balls

n red balls

(b) If there are n red balls in the arrangement, write down an expression for the number of black balls.

(c) If there are p black balls in an arrangement of this kind, write down an expression for the number of red balls.

7.2 (a) A box which weighs b kg empty contains n tins of paint, each weighing w kg. Write an expression for the total weight of the box and the tins of paint.

(b) A box of tennis balls weighs f kg when full of tennis balls and e kg when empty. There are n tennis balls in the box. Write an expression for the weight of one tennis ball.

7.3 A man leaves £a in his will, to be shared equally between his n children. Each child has to pay £1 in gift tax. Write an expression for the amount each child has after paying the tax.

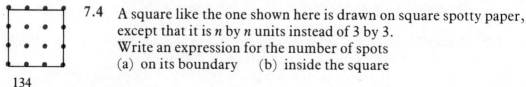

7.4 A square like the one shown here is drawn on square spotty paper, except that it is n by n units instead of 3 by 3. Write an expression for the number of spots
(a) on its boundary   (b) inside the square

7.5 A small tin of milk weighs 170 g and costs 25p. A large tin weighs 410 g and costs 54p. I buy a small tins and b large tins.

Write down an expression for
(a) the total weight in grams   (b) the total cost in pence
(c) the amount of change I would get from £5

7.6 Water flows from a tap at a constant rate. x litres of water come out in y minutes. Write an expression for

(a) the rate of flow in litres per minute
(b) the rate of flow in litres per second
(c) the number of litres which come out in 1 hour

8 Techniques of algebra

8.1 If $a = 5$, $b = 2$ and $c = {}^-3$, calculate

(a) $a^2 + bc$ (b) $a - bc$ (c) $5b^2$ (d) $a(b - c)$ (e) $b^2 - 3c$
(f) $\dfrac{b - c}{a}$ (g) $\left(\dfrac{a - c}{b}\right)^2$ (h) $ab - c^2$ (i) $\dfrac{a}{b} + c$ (j) $\dfrac{a}{b + c}$

8.2 Calculate the value of $(3r - 4s)^2$ when
(a) $r = 5$, $s = 2$ (b) $r = 0\cdot5$, $s = 0\cdot6$ (c) $r = 1\cdot5$, $s = {}^-0\cdot5$

8.3 A printer was asked to print some equations. He was not able to print brackets so he just left them out. In each equation, p is 2, q is 3 and r is 7. Re-write them with brackets where necessary.

(a) $pqr + p = 46$ (b) $pq + qr = 48$ (c) $p + qp^2 = 64$
(d) $q + qr^2 = 150$ (e) $2q^2 + r = 43$ (f) $pr + qp^2 = 68$

8.4 If $k = 0\cdot6$, $l = 2\cdot3$, $m = 1\cdot9$ and $n = 5\cdot5$, calculate to 1 d.p.

(a) kl^2 (b) $\dfrac{km}{ln}$ (c) $2m^2 - 3k^2$ (d) $\dfrac{l}{m} + \dfrac{n}{k}$ (e) $\dfrac{n^2}{kml}$

8.5 If $p = 3\cdot6 \times 10^5$, $q = 1\cdot3 \times 10^{-4}$ and $r = 7\cdot0 \times 10^{-8}$, calculate the value of each of these, to 2 significant figures.

(a) pq (b) qr (c) q^2 (d) $\dfrac{p}{q}$ (e) $\dfrac{pr}{q}$ (f) $\dfrac{q}{pr}$

8.6 Multiply out the brackets in each of these expressions.
(a) $3(p + q)$ (b) $3(p + 2q)$ (c) $5(a - 3)$ (d) $a(b - a)$ (e) $xy(x + y)$

8.7 Simplify each of these expressions, where possible.
(a) $3n + 5 - 2n + 2$ (b) $5x - 3y - 12x - 4y$ (c) $a + 4 - 9 - 3a$
(d) $2b - 3c - 5 + a$ (e) $7u - 8 + 1 - 5u$ (f) $10 - 2x - 5 + 6x$
(g) $ab - 2a + a^2 + b^2$ (h) $3ab + 2a^2 + 5ab - a^2$

8.8 Remove the brackets from these expressions. Simplify if possible.
   (a) $3x + (5 - x)$ (b) $4x + 6 - (2 + 3x)$ (c) $10 - (2x - 3)$
   (d) $3x + 2(4 + x)$ (e) $6x - 3(x + 2)$ (f) $20 + 5(a - 4)$
   (g) $11 - 3(2 - 4x)$ (h) $p^2 - p(q - p)$ (i) $5(2x - 3) - 2(3x - 1)$

8.9 Factorise each of these expressions.
   (a) $3a + 6b$ (b) $4a - 12$ (c) $ab^2 + 5b$ (d) $8ab - 2a^2$ (e) $p^2q - pq^2$

8.10 Multiply out the brackets in each of these expressions.
   (a) $(x + 3)(y + 5)$ (b) $(x + 5)(2x + 1)$ (c) $(3x + 2)(2x - 5)$
   (d) $(3x - 4)^2$ (e) $(5x + 2)(5x - 2)$ (f) $(4 - 5x)^2$

8.11 Factorise each of these expressions.
   (a) $x^2 + 7x + 12$ (b) $x^2 - 2x - 15$ (c) $x^2 + x - 20$ (d) $x^2 - 6x + 8$

8.12 Write each of these as a single algebraic fraction.
   (a) $\frac{a}{b} \times \frac{c}{d}$ (b) $\frac{4}{x} \times \frac{x}{y}$ (c) $\left(\frac{x+y}{3}\right) \times \frac{2}{x}$ (d) $\frac{a}{2} \div \frac{b}{3}$ (e) $\dfrac{\left(\frac{a}{3x}\right)}{\left(\frac{b}{12x}\right)}$

8.13 Write each of these as a single algebraic fraction.
   (a) $\frac{5}{a} + \frac{2}{b}$ (b) $\frac{r}{s} - \frac{2r}{st}$ (c) $\frac{x}{3a} - \frac{y}{a^2}$ (d) $\frac{5}{x-2} + \frac{3}{x}$ (e) $5x - \frac{3}{x}$

9 Solving equations and manipulating formulas

9.1 Solve each of these equations.
   (a) $3x - 17 = 28$ (b) $51 = 23 + 4x$ (c) $5x + 25 = 5$
   (d) $8x + 13 = 5x + 4$ (e) $6 - 3x = 2x - 4$ (f) $7 - x = 19 - 5x$

9.2 Solve each of these equations.
   (a) $\frac{3x - 2}{4} = 7$ (b) $2(3x - 1) = 16$ (c) $x = \frac{6 - x}{3}$

9.3 Solve these equations. Give the value of x to 2 d.p.
   (a) $2 \cdot 9x = 11 \cdot 3$ (b) $0 \cdot 83x = 0 \cdot 36$ (c) $\frac{x}{1 \cdot 6} = 0 \cdot 28$ (d) $\frac{3 \cdot 5}{x} = 0 \cdot 56$

9.4 P, V, R and T are connected by the equation $PV = RT$.
   (a) Write a formula for P in terms of the other letters.
   (b) Write a formula for V in terms of the other letters.
   (c) Write a formula for R in terms of the other letters.

9.5 u, v and m are connected by the formula $m = \frac{u}{v}$.
   (a) Re-arrange the formula to make u the subject.
   (b) Re-arrange the formula to make v the subject.

9.6 a, b, c and d are connected by the formula $d = ab + c$.
   (a) Calculate b, when $d = 37$, $a = 5$ and $c = 2$.
   (b) Calculate a, when $d = 13$, $b = 4$ and $c = 3$.
   (c) Re-arrange the formula so that c is the subject.
   (d) Re-arrange the formula so that a is the subject.

9.7 p, q, r and s related by the formula $r = \dfrac{p}{q} - s$.

   (a) Calculate p, when $r = 40$, $q = 3$ and $s = 2$.
   (b) Calculate s, when $r = 29$, $p = 10$ and $q = 2$.
   (c) Make p the subject of the formula.
   (d) Make s the subject of the formula.

9.8   Albert is 5 times as old as Gladys now. In 6 years' time, Albert
   will be only twice as old as Gladys.
   Let x stand for Gladys's age now.

   (a) Write an expression for Albert's age now, in terms of x.
   (b) Write expressions for Gladys's age and for Albert's age in 6 years' time.
   (c) Write an equation which says that in 6 years' time, Albert will be
        twice as old as Gladys. Solve the equation to find Gladys's age now.

9.9   Anne has six times as much money as Mark. If she gives
   Mark £10 then she will have twice as much as Mark.
   Solve an equation to find how much Mark has now.

9.10   Solve these equations. Give the value of x to 1 d.p.
   (a) $3 \cdot 2x - 0 \cdot 8 = 5 \cdot 1$ (b) $6 \cdot 7 - 1 \cdot 8x = 8 \cdot 5$ (c) $6 \cdot 1 = 8 \cdot 5 - 0 \cdot 3x$

9.11   Solve these equations.
   (a) $(x + 3)(x + 2) = x^2 + 24$ (b) $x(x - 3) = (x + 3)^2$

9.12   Make the letter printed in red the subject of each formula.
   (a) $s = \dfrac{ap}{qr}$ (b) $d = e - sf$ (c) $A = \dfrac{h(a + b)}{2}$ (d) $b = a(1 + rt)$

   (e) $a = \dfrac{v^2}{r}$ (f) $t = \sqrt{(au)}$ (g) $m = \dfrac{\sqrt{n}}{a}$ (h) $y = \sqrt{\left(\dfrac{a}{x}\right)}$

9.13   If $P = IV$ and $I = \dfrac{V}{R}$, find a formula for

   (a) P in terms of V and R (b) I in terms of P and V

   (c) V in terms of P and R (d) R in terms of P and V

9.14   If $x = 6y - z$ and $y = a + b$ and $z = 6 - b$, find a formula
   for x in terms of a and b, without brackets.

9.15   If $C = 2\pi r$ and $A = \pi r^2$, find a formula for A in terms of
   π and C.

9.16 Factorise the expression $x^2 + 5x + 6$, and use the result to solve the equation $x^2 + 5x + 6 = 0$.

9.17 Solve these equations by factorising.
(a) $x^2 - 2x - 8 = 0$
(b) $x^2 + x - 30 = 0$
(c) $x^2 - 5x = 0$
(d) $x^2 + 3x - 4 = 0$
(e) $x^2 - 8x + 15 = 0$
(f) $20 - 8x - x^2 = 0$

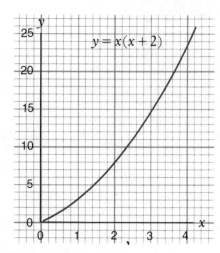

$y = x(x + 2)$

9.18 This is the graph of $y = x(x + 2)$ for values of x from 0 to 4.

(a) From the graph find, approximately, the value of x between 0 and 4 for which $x(x + 2) = 10$.

(b) Use the decimal search method to find this value, correct to 2 decimal places.

9.19 (a) Show that $x = 2 \cdot 6$ is an approximate solution of the equation $x^2 - x - 4 = 0$.

(b) Use the decimal search method to find this solution, correct to 2 d.p.

10 Linear equations and inequalities

10.1 Draw axes with x and y from $^-10$ to 10.
(a) Draw and label the line whose equation is $3x - 4y = 12$.
(b) The point $(1, 2)$ is above the line. Work out the value of $3x - 4y$ at $(1, 2)$.
(c) The point $(7, 0)$ is below the line. Work out the value of $3x - 4y$ at $(7, 0)$.
(d) Label clearly the region A where $3x - 4y < 12$, and the region B where $3x - 4y > 12$.
(e) Does the point $(6 \cdot 5, 1 \cdot 9)$ belong to region A or to region B?

10.2 If $p + q = 8$ and $3p + 4q = 31$, work out the values of

(a) $4p + 4q$
(b) $4p + 5q$
(c) $2p + 3q$
(d) $p + 2q$

10.3 If $r + 3s = 19$ and $5r + s = 18$, work out the values of

(a) $6r + 4s$
(b) $3r + 2s$
(c) $15r + 3s$
(d) $14r$

10.4 Find the common solution of each of these pairs of equations.
(a) $a + b = 23$
$a - b = 5$
(b) $5a + b = 15$
$3a + b = 7$
(c) $3x + 2y = 27$
$x + 3y = 16$
(d) $3p - 2q = 28$
$2p + 5q = 25$

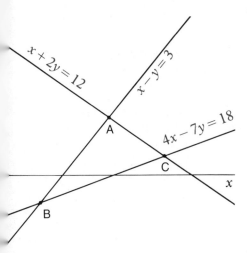

10.5 This diagram, which is not drawn accurately, shows the lines whose equations are

$$x - y = 3, \quad x + 2y = 12 \quad \text{and} \quad 4x - 7y = 18.$$

Calculate the coordinates of A, B and C.

10.6 In this pair of linear equations, a stands for a number.

$$x + 2y = 5$$
$$3x + 6y = a$$

What can you say about the solution of the equations

(a) when $a = 10$ (b) when $a = 15$

10.7 Draw axes with x and y from $^-5$ to 5.
Draw the line $2x - 3y = 6$. Indicate the region $2x - 3y < 6$ by shading out the unwanted part.

10.8 (a) State a pair of inequalities which together describe the region left unshaded in this diagram.

(b) Calculate the coordinates of the point A.

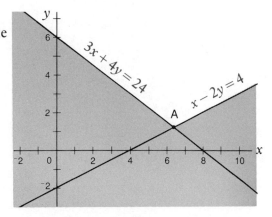

10.9 Which of these values of x fit the inequality $x^2 \geq {}^-4$?

(a) $^-2$ (b) 2   (c) 0   (d) -1

10.10 Solve these inequations

(a) $2x^2 < 32$ (b) $^-x^2 \leq 4$ (c) $^-x^2 > 0$ (d) $x^2 - 2x - 8 \geq 0$

(e) $x^2 + 3x < 4$ (f) $x^2 < 5x$ (g) $x^2 + 5x > {}^-6$ (h) $\dfrac{x^2}{2} \leq 4$

10.11 Find all the whole-number solutions to each of these.

(a) $0 \leq x < 4$ (b) $^-2 \leq x \leq {}^-1$ (c) $^-10 \leq 2x \leq {}^-6$

11 Graphs and functions

11.1 Karl is learning how to change the tyre on a wheel of a car.
As he does the job more and more often, he gets faster at it.
But eventually he gets to a point where he cannot do it any faster.

Sketch a graph showing how the time he takes to change a tyre
is related to the number of times he has done the job.
Draw axes like these.

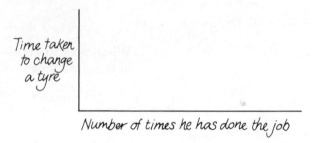

11.2 This sketch graph shows the amount of petrol in a car's tank
during a journey.

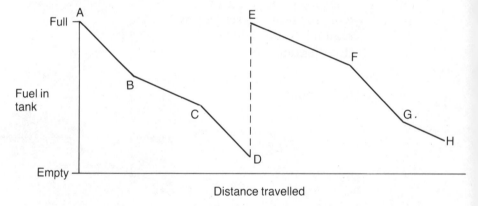

The journey involved two kinds of driving: in towns and on main roads.
In towns the car does fewer miles to a gallon than on main roads.

(a) Which parts of the graph show driving in towns? Explain how
you decide.

(b) What does the dotted line DE show?

11.3 A boy leans out of a balcony and throws a ball upwards.
The height of the ball above the ground is given by the formula
$h = 25 + 20t - 5t^2$, where t is the time in seconds since the ball
was thrown and h is the height of the ball above the ground, in metres.

(a) Draw a graph of (t, h) for values of t from 0 to 5.
(b) Use the graph to find the length of time for which the ball
was higher than 30 m above the ground.

140

11.4 For each graph shown below, write down
(i) its gradient (ii) its intercept on the y-axis (iii) its equation

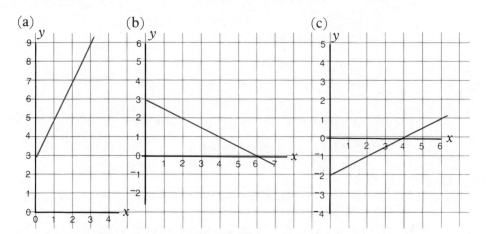

11.5 Draw axes with x and y from $^-5$ to 5.
(a) At each of these points, mark the value of $2x - 7y$ at that point:
$(0, 1)$, $(4, 1)$, $(2, 4)$, $(7, 3)$.
(b) Draw the line $2x - 7y = ^-7$.
(c) What is the gradient of the line?
(d) What is its intercept on the y-axis?
(e) Write down its equation, in the form $y = ax + b$.
(f) Use algebra to re-write the equation $2x - 7y = ^-7$ in the
form $y = ax + b$ and check that your answer agrees with
the answer to part (e).

11.6 The electrical resistance of a piece of wire increases as its
temperature increases.
A student did an experiment to investigate the relationship
between resistance and temperature. Here are her results.

T (temperature in °C)	20	30	50	70	80	100
R (resistance in ohms)	25·0	26·1	27·8	30·2	30·9	33

(a) Draw axes with T across (1 cm to 10 °C) and R up (1 cm
to 5 ohms). Plot the six points from the table.

(b) Draw a straight 'line of best fit' through the points. Find its
gradient and its intercept on the R-axis.

(c) Write the equation of your line of best fit.

11.7 Let s stand for the function $x \rightarrow 5 - 3x$.
(a) Calculate (i) s(3) (ii) s(0) (iii) s($^-$4)
(b) For which value of x is $s(x) = 20$?
(c) For which value of x is $s(x) = x$?

141

11.8 t is the function $x \rightarrow (x+1)(x-5)$.

(a) Copy and complete this table of values of t(x).

x	$(x+1)$	$(x-5)$	$t(x)$
$^-3$	$^-2 \quad \times$	$^-8$	16
$^-2$			
$^-1$			

(b) Draw a graph of t(x).

(c) Use the graph to answer this question: between which two values of x is $(x+1)(x-5) < 5$?

up to 7

(d) What are the two values of x for which $(x+1)(x-5) = 0$?

(e) Explain how you can work out the values of x for which $(x+1)(x-5) = 0$ without drawing a graph.

11.9 Work out where the graph of $x \rightarrow (x-2)(x-6)$ crosses the x-axis.

11.10 Where does each of these graphs cross the x-axis?

(a) $x \rightarrow x(x-4)$ (b) $x \rightarrow (x+3)(x+10)$ (c) $x \rightarrow (x-1)(x+5)$

11.11 Which of the drawings below could be a sketch of the graph of

(a) $y = \dfrac{x^2}{2}$ (b) $y = 5 - \dfrac{x}{2}$ (c) $y = \dfrac{2}{x}$ (d) $y = \dfrac{x}{2}$

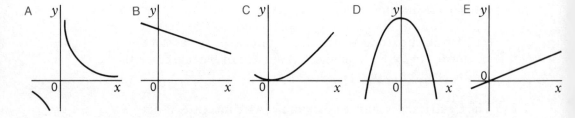

11.12 The values of p and q in this table are believed to fit an equation of the form $q = a \sqrt{p} + b$.

p	0·8	1·8	2·3	3·6	5·5	8·9
q	14·5	16·7	17·6	19·5	21·7	24·9

(a) Make a new table of values of $\sqrt{p}$ and q.

(b) Draw a graph and from it find a and b.

11.13 The values of r and s in this table are believed to fit roughly an equation of the form $s = ar^2 + b$.

r	0·6	1·1	1·5	2·0	2·3	2·5
s	17·5	16·2	14·6	12·0	10·1	8·6

By drawing a suitable graph, find values for a and b.

11.14 This graph shows the speed of a coach as it slows down to a stop. Calculate approximately the distance travelled during the 10 seconds shown on the graph, and describe your method of calculation.

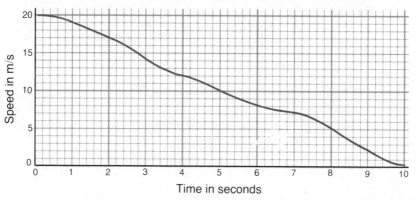

12 Proportionality

12.1 A shop sells silver braid. The cost of the braid is proportional to the length bought. You can buy 40 cm for £1·00.

(a) What will be the cost of   (i) 120 cm   (ii) 30 cm   (iii) 90 cm
(b) How much braid will you get for   (i) £5   (ii) £2·50   (iii) £25

12.2 Two towers stand side by side.
One tower is 32·5 m high and casts a shadow 45·1 m long.
The second tower's shadow is 58·3 m long.

(a) Calculate the multiplier from the first shadow to the second shadow.

(b) Calculate the height of the second tower, to the nearest 0·1 m.

12.3 A firm sells copper tubing of diameter 2·0 cm. The weight of a piece of this tubing is proportional to its length, and the cost is also proportional to the length.
A piece 30 cm long weighs 250 g and costs 48p.

(a) Calculate the weight and the cost of a 50 cm piece.
(b) What length can you buy for £10?

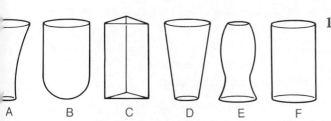

12.4 In which of these containers will the volume of liquid be proportional to depth?

A   B   C   D   E   F

12.5 A student studying electricity varied the voltage across a piece of wire and measured the current in the wire each time. Here are her results. V stands for the voltage, in volts, and I for the current, in amps.

V	1·5	2·2	3·2	4·3	5·0
I	3·9	5·7	8·3	11·2	13·0

(a) Draw axes with V across and I up. Plot the five points, and draw the graph of (V, I).
(b) Is I proportional to V? How can you tell from the graph?
(c) Find the gradient of the graph.
(d) Write down the equation connecting I and V in the form $I = \ldots V$.

12.6 Find the equation connecting y and x for each of these graphs.

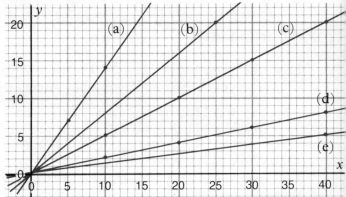

12.7 A van which travels at an average speed of 27 m.p.h. can cover the distance from London to Barnsley in $6\frac{1}{2}$ hours.
(a) What is the average speed of a coach which can do the same trip in $3\frac{1}{4}$ hours?
(b) How long would the journey take in a veteran car with an average speed of 9 m.p.h.?

12.8 If a beam of a certain cross-section is supported at both ends, the weight, W kg, it can carry at its centre is inversely proportional to its length, l cm.

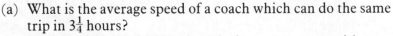

If $W = 1·6$ when $l = 25$, calculate

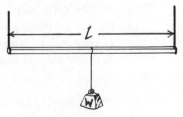

(a) W when $l = 12·5$ (b) W when $l = 40$ (c) l when $W = 2·5$

12.9 The weight, W kg, which can be supported by a certain kind of rope is proportional to the square of its diameter, d mm. When d is 12, then W is 2500. Calculate, to 2 s.f.,
(a) W when $d = 22$ (b) W when $d = 10$

144

13 Exponential growth and decay

13.1 When Sadia was born, several relatives gave money for her, amounting to £50 altogether. Sadia's mother put the money into a savings account where the rate of interest was 8% p.a. On Sadia's 18th birthday, her mother told her about the account. Calculate the amount in the account by then.

13.2 An oven is switched off, opened, and allowed to cool.
The temperature afterwards is given by the formula $T = 15 + 200 \times 4^{-t}$.
T stands for the temperature in °C, and t for the time in minutes since the oven was switched off.

(a) Calculate T when t is 0, 1, 2, 3 and 4.

(b) Draw a graph of (t, T). What happens to T as t increases?

14 Sequences and iteration

14.1 The nth term of a sequence a is given by the formula $a_n = \dfrac{n(n+1)}{2}$.

(a) Write down the values of a_1, a_2, a_3, a_4, a_5 and a_6.
(b) What name is given to this sequence?

14.2 Find a formula for the nth term of the arithmetic sequence $3, 7, 11, 15, \ldots$

14.3 The sequence u is an arithmetic sequence. $u_1 = 5$ and $u_2 = 11$.
(a) Write down the value of u_3.
(b) Find a formula for u_n in terms of n.

14.4 This pattern of short and tall houses continues along a street. Find a formula for the number of the nth tall house.

14.5 Find a formula for the nth term of the geometric sequence $3, 12, 48, 192, \ldots$

14.6 (a) Write down the values of d_1 to d_6 produced by this flowchart.

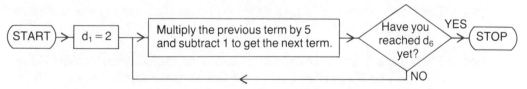

(b) Write down the formula connecting d_n and d_{n+1}.

14.7 v is a sequence whose first term v_1 is 8. The formula connecting v_n and v_{n+1} is $v_{n+1} = 2v_n + 3$. Write down the values of v_2, v_3, v_4 and v_5.

14.8 The sequence d starts $3, 8, 23, 68, \ldots$ The formula connecting d_n and d_{n+1} is of the form $d_{n+1} = ad_n + b$. Find a and b.

14.9 Let r_n be the number of dots in the nth 'ring' of dots in this diagram.
(For example, $r_1 = 4$ and $r_2 = 12$.)

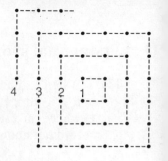

(a) Find the formula connecting r_n and r_{n+1}.

(b) Find the formula for r_n in terms of n.

14.10 The iteration formula for a sequence u is $u_{n+1} = \dfrac{3u_n + 1}{2}$.

(a) Starting with $u_1 = 5$, calculate u_2, u_3, u_4 and u_5.
(b) Does the sequence appear to converge when $u_1 = 5$?
(c) Calculate the fixed point of the iteration formula (the value of u_1 for which $u_1 = u_2 = u_3 = u_4 = \ldots$).

14.11 The iteration formula for a sequence u is $u_{n+1} = \dfrac{3u_n + 1}{5}$.

(a) Starting with $u_1 = 1$, calculate u_2, u_3, u_4 and u_5.
(b) Does the sequence appear to converge when $u_1 = 1$?
(c) Calculate the fixed point of the iteration formula.

15 Number properties

15.1 Solve this equation which was set for students in the 16th century.
'Find me a number such that when it is cubed, and the said number added to this cube, the result is close to five.'

15.2 What is the smallest number you can find which is divisible by 2, 3, 4, 5, 6, 7, 8, 9 and 10?

15.3 Work this out on your calculator: $\left(\dfrac{2143}{22}\right)^{\frac{1}{4}}$

What is the difference between this and π to 4 d.p.?

15.4 The formula $y = x(x - 1) + 41$ seems to generate only prime numbers. Is this true? Why?

15.5 There are at least two expressions involving indices which have a value of 81, 9^2 and 3^4. Find as many expressions as you can involving indices which have a value of 256.

15.6 Explain why all square numbers have an odd number of factors.

16 Loci

16.1 This is a plan of a back garden, drawn to a scale of $\frac{1}{2}$ cm to 1 m.

Copy the plan and colour the part of the garden which cannot be seen from the window.

16.2 Two farmers living at A and B agree to dig a well and share it.

The well must be the same distance from A and from B, but it must be dug on land no higher than 10 m above sea-level.

(a) Trace or copy the map and show the possible positions of the well.

(b) Mark with a W the position which is closest to the farmhouses.

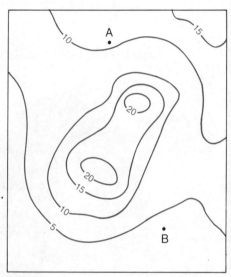

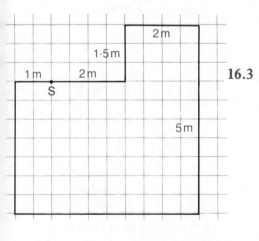

16.3 The plan on the left shows a room with only one electric socket (S).

A standard lamp has a lead which is 3 m long. Draw the room plan to scale and shade the area where you could put the lamp and be able to plug it in.

16.4 This is an island with three schools P, Q and R. Children living on the island go to the nearest school.

Draw the map and divide the island up between the three schools. Which school serves the largest area?

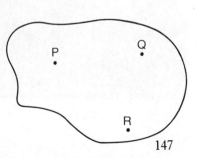

147

17 Pythagoras' rule

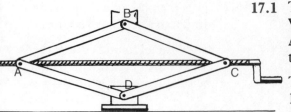

17.1 This diagram shows a type of car jack. When the handle is turned, the points A and C move closer together, and the point B rises.

The lengths AB, BC, CD and DA are each 15 cm. Calculate the height of B above D when AC is 22 cm.

17.2 The three corners of a triangle are at A(1, 0), B(7, 3) and C(3, 8). Calculate the length of   (a) AB   (b) BC   (c) CA

18 The circle: circumference and area

WIEN, PRATER, RIESENRAD   27656

18.1 This is an old photograph of the Giant Wheel in Vienna.

(a) How many cars are there round the edge of the wheel?

(b) Each car is about 2·5 m tall, and hangs from a pivot.

From the photo, estimate the distance between pivots.

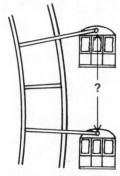

(c) Use your estimate in (b) to estimate the circumference of the wheel.

(d) Hence estimate the diameter of the wheel.

18.2   Calculate these. Give each answer correct to 3 s.f.

    (a)   The area of a circle of radius 6·55 m

    (b)   The circumference of a circle of radius 2·93 m

    (c)   The radius of a circle of area 0·85 m²

    (d)   The area of a circle of circumference 13·7 m

18.3   A circular saw is rotating at a speed of 100 revolutions per minute. The diameter of the saw is 35 cm.

    (a)   How far does a point on the edge of the saw travel in one minute?

    (b)   Calculate the speed of a point on the edge of the saw, in cm/s, to the nearest 10 cm/s.

19   Angle relationships

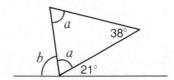

19.1   The angles marked a in this diagram are equal. Calculate a and b.

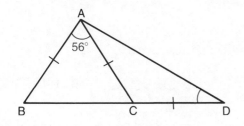

19.2   In the diagram on the left AB = AC = CD.

Calculate the angle marked x.

Explain each step of your working.

19.3   ABC is a triangle The side BC is extended to form the **exterior angle** at C (marked x).

Explain why $x = a + b$.

(You may find it helpful to add an extra line through C, parallel to BA, as shown below.)

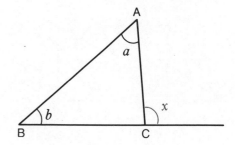

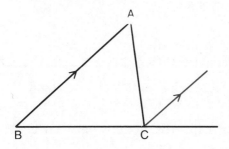

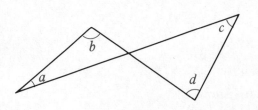

19.4 Show that, in the diagram on the left,

$$a + b = c + d.$$

19.5 This diagram shows part of a regular polygon.

How many sides does the polygon have?

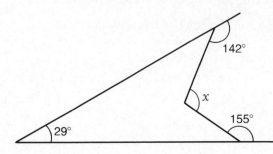

160°

142°

x

155°

29°

19.6 Calculate the angle marked *x* in the diagram on the left.

Explain each step of your working.

20 Mappings and symmetry

20.1 Which of these 'words' have a 2-fold rotation centre?

(a) pod   (b) shoys   (c) bozzop   (d) onzuo

(e) dollop   (f) hoxoy   (g) poqdob   (h) snous

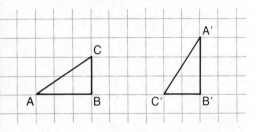

A'   C   A   B   C'   B'

20.2 Draw diagrams to show how to map triangle ABC onto A′B′C′ by

(a) a rotation about one of the corner point A, B, D followed by a reflection

(b) reflection in a line through C followed by a translation

20.3 Draw the triangle ABC. Let angle CAB be *a*°.

(a) Reflect the triangle in the line AB. Draw the image and label it AB′C′.

(b) Rotate triangle AB′C′ through *a*° anticlockwise about A. Draw the image and label it AB″C″.

(c) Which single mapping maps ABC directly onto AB″C″? Describe it as precisely as you can.

C

A   *a*°   B

21 Trigonometry

21.1 Calculate the lengths marked with letters. (All measurements in cm.)

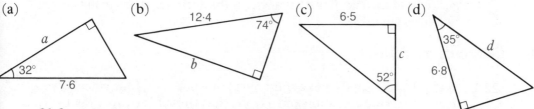

(a)

(b)

(c)

(d)

21.2 Calculate the angles marked with letters.

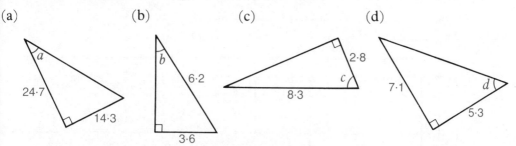

(a)

(b)

(c)

(d)

21.3 A straight roadway is 10·4 m wide. If you walk across it at an angle of 35° to an edge of the roadway, how far do you walk?

21.4 The diagram on the right shows the symmetrical cross-section of a railway embankment.

Calculate the angle which each sloping edge makes with the horizontal.

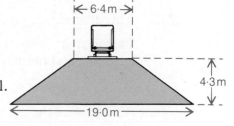

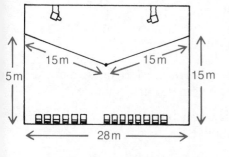

21.5 A microphone is hung from the sides of a school hall, as shown in this drawing.

(a) Calculate the angle which each of the two wires makes with the horizontal.

(b) Calculate the height of the microphone above the floor of the hall.

21.6 (a) Find two values of x in the range 0° to 360° for which $\sin x = 0·4$. (Give each angle to the nearest 0·1°.)

(b) Find two values of x in the range 0° to 360° for which $\cos x = {}^-0·8$.

21.7 (a) Sketch on the same axes the graphs of $y = \sin x$ and $y = \cos x$ for values of x from 0° to 360°.

(b) For which values of x between 0° and 360° is $\sin x$ equal to $\cos x$?

21.8 Use trial and improvement to find the largest possible value of sin x × cos x.

21.9 The formula $\tan x \approx \dfrac{x}{57}$ gives a good approximation for small positive values of x. For what angles is this formula accurate to two significant figures?

22 Three dimensions

22.1 A child's toy consists of a solid block of wood with four wheels. Here are a side elevation and a front elevation of the toy, drawn to a scale of 1 cm to 10 cm.

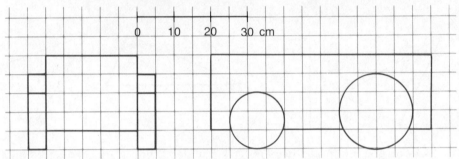

Draw, to the same scale, a plan view of the toy.

22.2 This drawing shows the roof of a small shelter.

Imagine that the roof is cut along the edge AB, and flattened out to make a net.

(a) Draw the net to a scale of 1 cm to 1 m.

(b) Measure the net to find the area of the roof. Explain how you do it.

(c) Use the net to measure the shortest distance on the surface of the roof from one corner to the corner opposite.

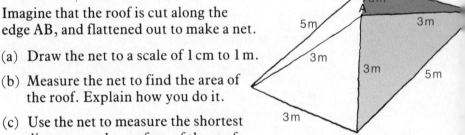

22.3

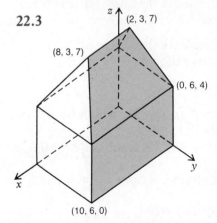

The diagram on the left shows a house. All measurements are in metres.

The diagrams below show two elevations of the house.

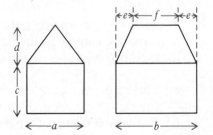

152

(a) Work out the lengths marked a, b, c, d, e and f.

(b) The 'roof-space' of the house can be divided into three sections, A, B and C, as shown in this diagram.

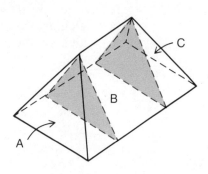

If part B is removed, and parts A and C are moved together so that the red triangles coincide, what kind of solid will A and C together make?

(c) Calculate the **total** volume of the roof-space, showing your method clearly.

[Volume of pyramid $= \frac{1}{3} \times$ area of base $\times$ height.]

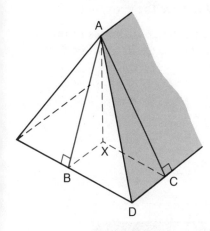

22.4 The diagram on the left shows an end of the same roof as shown above.

(a) Calculate AB.

(b) Calculate AC.

(c) Calculate AD.

(d) Calculate the **total area** of the roof of the house, showing your method clearly.

(e) Calculate the angle which the sloping edge AD makes with the horizontal.

22.5 These drawings show a sketch and three views of a tent. One triangular panel is shown shaded. Its edges are a, b and c.

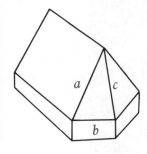

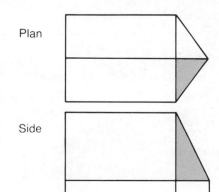

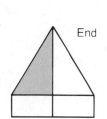

Make rough copies of the three views.

In which view does edge a appear correctly to scale, so that you could measure its length from the view? Mark the edge with an a in that view. Then do the same for edge b and edge c.

22.6 The helix shown here divides the curved surface of the cylinder into two parts, black and white.
(a) Calculate the area of the black part.
(b) Calculate the length of the helix.

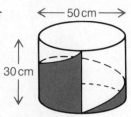

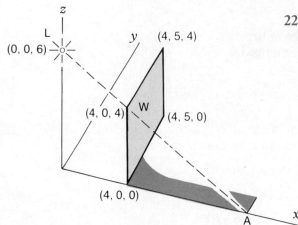

22.7 A light is situated at L.
The vertical wall W casts a shadow on the horizontal ground.

Part of the shadow is shown.
A is one corner of it.

(a) What are the coordinates of A?

(b) Find the coordinates of the other corner(s) of the shadow.

23 Enlargement and reduction

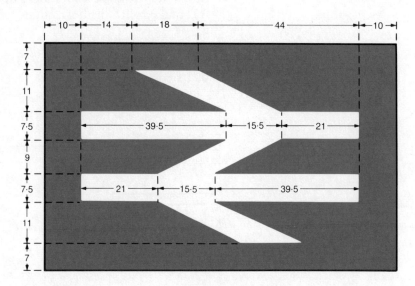

23.1 The dimensions on this drawing are in millimetres. Suppose the drawing is enlarged so that the red rectangle is 144 mm high.

(a) Calculate the scale factor of the enlargement.
(b) How long will the red rectangle be in the enlargement?
(c) How long and how wide will each horizontal bar be?

154

23.2 A church council has commissioned a sculptor to make a stone statue of an angel. The statue is to be painted gold. The sculptor has made a model of the statue, also in stone. The model is 25 cm high, weighs 6·4 kg and needs 0·15 litre of gold paint.

The real statue is to be 2·0 metres high.

(a) How much will the real statue weigh?
(b) How much gold paint will be needed to paint it?

23.3 Blagdon Zoo covers an area of 85 500 m². Inside the zoo is a model zoo. The model is a model of Blagdon Zoo itself, and is made to a scale of 2 cm to 1 m.

(a) Calculate the area of the model zoo, in m².
(b) Inside the model zoo is a model of the model zoo. Calculate the area of this model, in cm².

24 Dimensions of units

24.1 The base of a skewed pyramid has area a and the top has height h. Which of these formulas could give the volume of the pyramid?

(a) $\frac{1}{3}a^2h$ (b) $\frac{1}{3}ah$

24.2 Could this formula be correct?

'The area of a rhombus whose one side is length a and whose two diagonals are of length b and c is $\sqrt{(abc)}$.'

25 Statistics

25.1 A firm sells paper clips in boxes marked 'about 100'. To check the contents, a sample of 20 boxes were opened and the clips counted.

Number of clips in box	95	96	97	98	99	100	101	102
Number of boxes	1	2	4	4	7	1	0	1

Calculate the mean number of paper clips per box in the sample.

25.2 Large samples of two species of snake were caught and the length of each snake was measured. The cumulative frequency graphs of the lengths in each species (A and B) are shown below.

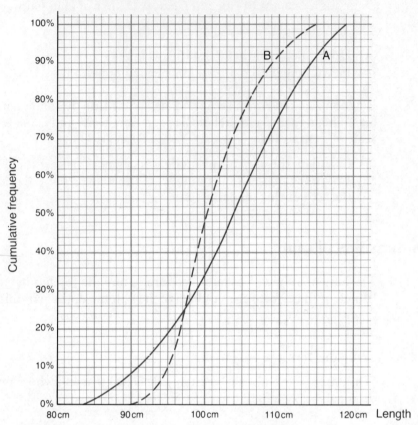

(a) What is the range of lengths in each species?

(b) What is the median length in each species?

(c) What percentage of species A were more than 1 metre in length?

(d) What percentage of species B were more than 1 metre in length?

(e) Calculate the interquartile range of each species.

(f) If you compare the interquartile ranges, what does that tell you about the distribution of lengths in the two species?

(g) Copy and complete this percentage frequency table.

(h) From the information in your table, draw two frequency charts, one for each species. Lay them out on the page so that they can easily be compared.

Length in cm	Percentage of species A	Percentage of species B
80–85	2%	0%
85–90	7%	0%
90–95	10%	10%
⋮	⋮	⋮
115–120		

25.3 Two wine 'experts' were asked to rate the quality of 15 different types of wine and to give each wine a score out of 10. Here are their scores.

Wine	A	B	C	D	E	F	G	H	I	J	K	L	M	N	O
1st expert	6	4	6	3	8	1	8	8	9	4	2	5	4	3	7
2nd expert	8	3	6	4	9	2	1	8	8	4	3	5	5	3	6

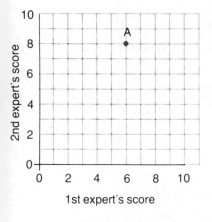

(a) Draw axes as shown on the left. Mark each pair of scores as a point on the diagram.

(b) Look at the diagram. Is there any particular wine which the experts disagree about very strongly? If so, which wine is it?

(c) Apart from this wine, is there a reasonable amount of agreement between the experts?

(d) Where would the points lie if the experts agreed on the score for every one of the wines?

(e) Calculate the mean of the scores given by the first expert. Do the same for the second expert. Which expert gave higher scores on average?

(f) Calculate the standard deviations of the scores.

(g) The magazine which asked the experts to rate the wines wants to print an 'order of merit', showing the 15 wines in order of quality, best first. Suggest how they might make an 'order of merit'.

25.4 This table shows the lengths in seconds (t) of the telephone calls made by a business over a few weeks. 200–300 stands for $200 \le t < 300$.

Length of call (t) in seconds	0–100	100–200	200–300	300–400	400–500	500–600
Frequency	7	23	89	182	244	262
Length of call (t) in seconds	600–700	700–800	800–900	900–1000	1000–1100	
Frequency	135	43	9	4	2	

(a) Show this information on a frequency graph.

(b) Find the mean length of a telephone call.

(c) What is the standard deviation?

25.5 A biologist in experimenting with a new fertiliser. Two boxes, A and B, each containing a row of 14 seedlings, were placed side by side in a greenhouse.
Each box is treated the same but Box B is given the new fertiliser.
For each plant the number of days before matures is noted.
Here are the results:

Box A	70	65	64	66	67	63	62	62	68	65	65	64	64	64
Box B	65	65	64	63	60	60	60	64	61	61	64	60	63	64

Did the new fertiliser have any effect on the growth of the plants?
Give reasons for your answers.

25.6 This table shows the pH value of the water in a river each day for a month.

6·7	6·3	6·2	6·1	7·0	7·0	7·2
6·3	6·4	7·1	7·0	7·0	6·8	6·9
6·4	6·3	6·3	6·1	7·0	6·4	5·9
6·1	6·3	6·0	6·1	6·3	7·1	6·9

Use a calculator to obtain the mean and standard deviation of these 28 readings.

26 Selections and arrangements

26.1 A salesman starts from town S and goes on a tour, visiting each of the other towns once. One possible order for visiting them is CADB. How many different possible orders are there?

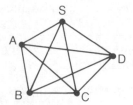

26.2 Stevie's Jeans are made in these waist measurements
     26   28   30   32   34   36   38
and in these inside leg measurements
     27   29   31   33

(a) The factory makes jeans with every different possible combination of measurements, e.g. waist 38, inside leg 29.
How many possible combinations are there?

(b) Stevie's decide to include a waist measurement of 40 in their range and also an inside leg measurement of 25.
They manufacture every possible combination **except** waist 40 with inside leg 25. How many possible combinations are there?

26.3 A, B, C, D, E, F, G and H are eight people. B, C and G are friendly with each other. A is friendly with D, with E and with H. F is friendly with B, D, E and H.

Can all eight people sit in a row so that every person sits next to a friend?

If not, can they do it if one person drops out? If so, who could drop out, and who could sit at each end?

27 Probability

27.1 Audrey has five cards, numbered 1, 2, 3, 4, 5. She shuffles them and Kevin picks two cards at random.

(a) Make a list of all the possible pairs of cards Kevin could pick.

(b) What is the probability that Kevin picks a pair of consecutive numbers (e.g. 1 and 2, or 3 and 4, etc.)?

27.2 Calculate the probability of throwing four sixes in four throws of an ordinary dice.

27.3 Square sheets of plastic are fed into two cutting machines, one after the other. The first machine is supposed to cut each sheet in half 'across' and the second to cut in half 'down'.

The machines are independent of each other, but both are unreliable. It has been observed that the first machine fails to cut 1 sheet in 5, and the second fails to cut 1 sheet in 4.

If a sheet is fed into the machines, calculate the probability that it comes out   (a) not cut at all   (b) cut into halves   (c) cut into quarters

27.4 Stephanie has invented a game for Simon to play. Simon throws three coins. If they all land the same way (all heads or all tails) Stephanie pays Simon 10p. If they are not all the same, Simon throws them all again. This time if they are all the same, Stephanie pays him 5p. Otherwise he pays Stephanie 10p.

(a) Copy this tree diagram and write the probabilities on the branches.

(b) Calculate the probability that Simon
    (i) wins 10p
    (ii) wins 5p
    (iii) loses 10p

Coins same (Simon wins 10p.)

Same (Simon wins 5p.)

Coins not same

Not same (Simon loses 10p.)

(c) Simon plays 1000 times. About how much do you expect him to win or lose altogether?

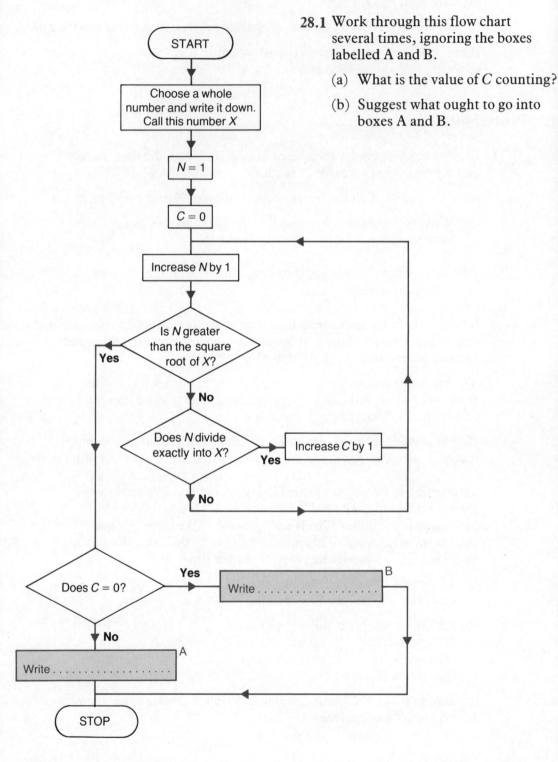

28.1 Work through this flow chart several times, ignoring the boxes labelled A and B.

(a) What is the value of C counting?

(b) Suggest what ought to go into boxes A and B.

Flow chart content:

START

Choose a whole number and write it down. Call this number X

$N = 1$

$C = 0$

Increase N by 1

Is N greater than the square root of X? — Yes

No

Does N divide exactly into X? — Yes → Increase C by 1

No

Does $C = 0$? — Yes → Write . . . . B

No — A

Write . . . .

STOP

M Miscellaneous questions

The questions in this section are taken from the SMP 11–16 pilot 16+ examination (papers 3 and 4) and are reprinted with the kind permission of the Oxford and Cambridge Schools Examination Board, and the East Anglian Examinations Board.

M1 Work out $\dfrac{43{\cdot}76 \times 0{\cdot}0163}{\sqrt{283{\cdot}71}}$.

(a) Write down all the figures in your calculator display.

(b) Write your answer to 3 significant figures.

M2 The speed of light in space is 299 800 000 m/s, to 4 significant figures.

Write this number in standard index form.

M3 Find the value of x if $\dfrac{450}{x} = 15$.

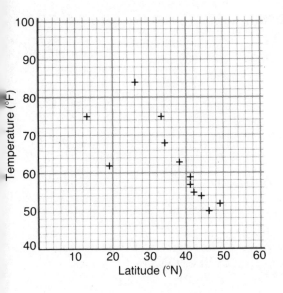

Temperature (°F) vs Latitude (°N)

M4 The maximum temperature in degrees Fahrenheit (°F) is recorded on a November day in twelve places in North America.

These temperatures are marked on this scatter diagram, together with the latitude of each place.

(The latitude, measured in degrees, tells you how far north a place is from the equator.)

What can you say about the relationship between latitude and temperature?

M5 Draw axes with x and y from $^-4$ to 10.
Draw a straight line through $(^-4, ^-3)$ and $(8, 3)$.

(a) What is the gradient of this line?

(b) Write down the equation of the line.

M6 Which of these is the smallest?
(a) 2^{16} (b) 4^8 (c) 8^4 (d) 16^2

M7 A 'penny farthing' bicycle has wheels of two different sizes.

Their diameters are 125 cm and 39·5 cm.

(a) Calculate the circumference of

  (i) the large wheel   (ii) the small wheel

(b) How far does the cycle travel as the large wheel makes 20 revolutions? Give your answer in **metres**.

(c) How many revolutions does the small wheel make in travelling the same distance?

M8 A piston fits tightly in a vertical cylinder, trapping the air below it.

When a weight w kg is placed on the piston, the height of the piston above the base is h m.

h is inversely proportional to w.

(a) Sketch a graph of (w, h) on axes like these.

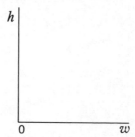

(b) What happens to h when w is halved?

(c) If $h = 45$ when $w = 250$, calculate h when $w = 300$.

M9 I travel to school by bus. Sometimes the bus arrives at the bus stop at the same time as I do. At other times I have to wait, for up to 10 minutes.

If the traffic lights are all green, the bus journey takes 7 minutes. Usually the journey takes longer, sometimes as long as 12 minutes.

It takes me 5 minutes to walk from home to the bus stop. It takes me 2 minutes to walk from the bus into school. I have to be in school by 8:45 a.m.

(a) By what time must I leave home to be **sure** of arriving at school on time?

(b) If I leave home at this time, what is the earliest I could arrive at school?

M10 (a) Write down the sum of the interior angles of a quadrilateral.

(b) Draw this pentagon.
Draw a diagonal in it.

Work out the sum of the interior
angles of the pentagon.

(c) Suppose that two of the interior angles of a pentagon are each 120°
and the other three angles are all equal to each other.
Work out the size of each of the other three angles.

M11 The frequency of a note played on the E-string of a violin
is **inversely** proportional to the length of
the vibrating part of the string.

(a) What happens to the frequency of the note when
the length of the vibrating part of the string is halved?

(b) Frequency is measured in hertz (Hz).
When the vibrating length is 204 mm, the frequency is 2048 Hz.
(i) Calculate the frequency when the length is 250 mm.
(ii) Calculate the length when the frequency is 3000 Hz.

M12 This diagram shows a cross-section of a symmetrical railway
embankment. It is in the shape of a trapezium.
The diagram is not to scale.

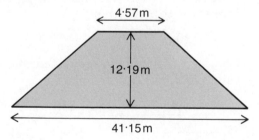

(a) (i) Calculate the area of the cross-section.

(ii) How many cubic metres of material
are required to build a 100 m
length of the embankment?

(b) This is a drawing of the
same cross-section.

(i) Calculate the length AB.

(ii) Calculate the angle θ.

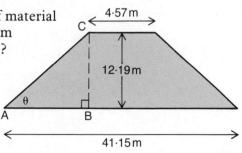

163

When measuring skid marks, the police can use this formula
to estimate the speed of the vehicle.

$$s = \sqrt{(30fd)}$$

s is the speed in miles per hour (m.p.h.).
d is the length of the skid, in feet.
f is a number which depends on the weather and the type of road.

This table shows some values of *f*.

		Road surface	
		Concrete	Tar
Weather	Wet	0·4	0·5
	Dry	0·8	1·0

(a) A car travelling on a wet concrete road makes a skid mark
of length 80 feet. How fast was it travelling?

(b) (i) When the road surface is tar and the weather is dry, the
formula may be written

$$s = \sqrt{(30d)}$$

Complete this table to show the values of *s* for the given
values of *d*, to 1 decimal place.

d	50	100	150	200	250
30*d*	1500				
$s = \sqrt{(30d)}$	38·7				

(ii) Draw axes, with *d* from 0 to 250 (use 2 cm for 50) and
s from 0 to 100 (use 1 cm for 10).
Draw the graph of (*d*, *s*).

(iii) Use your graph to find how many feet a car would skid on
a dry tar road at 75 m.p.h.

M14 In this question, you will need the formula

Surface area of disc $= 2\pi r(r + t)$

where r is the radius and t the thickness.

The disease *multiple mycloma* causes the red blood cells, which are like discs, to stick together (like a pile of coins).

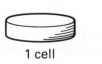

When the cells stick together, there are fewer faces to absorb oxygen.

1 cell

4 cells stuck together

The cells have a thickness of 2·2 microns and a diameter of 7·2 microns.

The surface area is measured in square microns.

(a) (i) What is the radius of a cell?

(ii) Find the surface area of one cell.

(iii) Find the total surface area of four separate cells.

(b) (i) Find the surface area of four cells stuck together.

(ii) Find the percentage decrease in surface area when four cells stick together.

M15 Work out $(4{\cdot}29 \times 10^{-7}) \times (2{\cdot}79 \times 10^{3})$.
Give your answer (a) in standard index form
(b) in ordinary decimal form

M16 This table gives the first four terms of a sequence u.

u_1	u_2	u_3	u_4	...
3	6	12	24	...

(a) There is a simple relationship connecting each term with the next one. What is the relationship? Write it in words or in symbols.

(b) Write down a formula for the nth term u_n in terms of n.

M17 For cars travelling at normal speed, the air drag is roughly proportional to SV^2, where S is the surface area of the car and V is the speed.

By what number will the air drag be multiplied when the car increases speed from 40 km/h to 120 km/h?

165

M18 Opticians use the formula $D = \dfrac{1}{u} + \dfrac{1}{v}$.

What can you say about the value of D if $v = 0{\cdot}02$ and u is approximately $1\,000\,000$?

M19 Solve the equation $x^2 - 3x - 10 = 0$.

M20 The mean weight of eight oarsmen is $78{\cdot}3\,\text{kg}$.
The ninth member of the crew weighs $48{\cdot}6\,\text{kg}$.

What is the mean weight of all nine?

M21 A vacuum pump is designed to remove 25% of the gas in a vacuum chamber with each stroke.

(a) What percentage of the gas will be left after
(i) 1 stroke (ii) 2 strokes

(b) How many strokes are needed to remove about 90% of the gas which was originally in the chamber?

M22 Roughly how many matchboxes of this size have a total volume of 1 cubic metre?

Show clearly how you get your estimate.

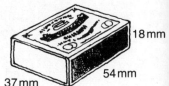

18 mm

54 mm

37 mm

M23 A sequence begins $1, 3, 7, 15, 31, 63, \cdots$
It has a simple term-to-term rule.

(a) Write down this rule in words.

(b) Use the rule to find the next term of the sequence.

(c) The nth term of the sequence is denoted by s_n.
Write the rule as an equation connecting s_{n+1} and s_n.

(d) Make a new sequence by adding 1 to each term of the sequence above
Write an expression in terms of n for the nth term of the new sequenc

(e) Use your answer to part (d) to write down a formula for
s_n in terms of n.

M24 x and y are given by these formulas.

$$x = pt \quad \text{and} \quad y = p(1 + qt)$$

(a) Find a formula for y in terms of p, q and x which does not include t.

(b) Find a formula for x in terms of p, q and y which does not include t.

M25 (a) A bank exchanges £ sterling for dollars at the rate of $1·39 for £1.
It deducts 5% for doing the work.
How much in dollars will I get for £200?

(b) Dollars may be exchanged for £ sterling at the rate of
$1·41 for £1. Again the deduction is 5%.
How much in £ sterling will I get for $260?

M26 A salesman reports an increase of 55% in his sales this year
compared with last year.

The increase was £43 197.
What were his actual sales this year?

M27 The iteration formula of a sequence u is

$$u_{n+1} = \frac{u_n - 1}{4}$$

(a) Starting with $u_1 = 5$, calculate u_2, u_3, u_4, u_5 and u_6.

(b) Guess the value of the limit towards which the sequence
seems to converge.

(c) Calculate the fixed point of the iteration formula
(the value of u_1 for which $u_1 = u_2 = u_3$ etc.).

M28 $y \propto \dfrac{1}{x^2}$

$y = 1·8$ when $x = 4$.

Find y when $x = 12$.

M29 A hospital keeps two types of glucose solution, weak and strong.

The weak solution contains 20 g of glucose per litre.
The strong solution contains 80 g of glucose per litre.

(a) Suppose x litres of the weak solution are mixed with y litres of the
strong solution.

Write an expression, in terms of x and y, for

(i) the total volume of the mixture, in litres

(ii) the amount of glucose in the mixture, in grams

(b) A nurse needs to mix the weak and strong solutions to make
6 litres of a new solution, containing 45 g of glucose per litre.

Calculate the volume of weak solution and the volume of strong
solution which she must mix together.

M30 What is the straight-line distance between $(7, 5)$ and $(1, {}^-3)$?

M31 Butter is to be supplied to Hillbury's Superstore in boxes containing 250 g packs of butter.

Each 250 g pack is a cuboid measuring 96 mm by 64 mm by 36 mm.

The internal dimensions of the boxes into which these are to be packed are 500 mm by 300 mm by 250 mm

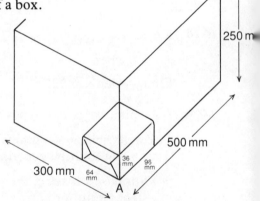

There are several different ways of placing one pack in the bottom corner of a box.

One way is like this.

We can represent this way of placing the pack by this symbol:

(a) Using similar symbols, list all the different ways of placing one pack in the bottom corner A of the box.

(b) When the packs of butter are put into the box they must all be the same way round. For each of the possibilities in (a), calculate how many packs can be fitted inside the box.

(c) (i) One of the solutions in part (b) gives the largest number of packs. Is it possible to make the box smaller and still contain this arrangement of packs? If so, what are the dimensions of the box which will just hold these packs?

(ii) Is this a solution which the superstore is likely to adopt? Give a reason for your answer.

M32 The digits 1, 2, 3, 4, 5, 6, 7, 8, 9 are each printed on a separate card and the nine cards are shuffled.

A card is chosen at random, looked at, and replaced.
Then the pack is shuffled again and a second card is chosen at random.

The first number chosen forms the 'tens' digit of a number, the second the 'units' digit.
For example, if 5 and then 6 are chosen, the number formed is 56.

(a) What is the probability that a number less than 20 is formed?

(b) What is the probability that the number 14 is formed?

M33 The face of Brian's watch is decorated with two circles and a square.

The shaded part is gold.

One side of the square measures 20·0 mm.

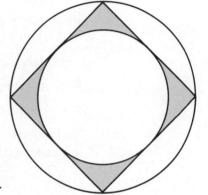

(a) What is the radius of the small circle?

(b) What is the area of gold?

(c) Calculate the radius of the large circle.

M34 Each shape below is made from a piece of wire of length 12 cm.
Calculate the area of each shape, to the nearest 0·1 cm^2.

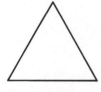

(a) Equilateral triangle   (b) Square   (c) Regular hexagon   (d) Circle

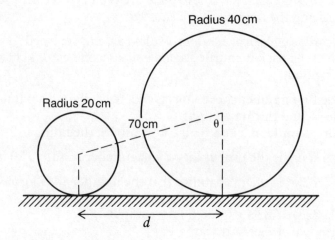

(a) This diagram shows two wheels, of radius 20 cm and 40 cm, standing on horizontal ground.

The distance between their centres is 70 cm.

  (i) Calculate the distance marked d.

  (ii) Calculate the angle marked θ.

(b) The same two wheels, with their centres still 70 cm apart, are connected by a tight belt, as shown below.

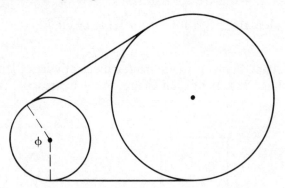

  (i) Draw the diagram and add the line of symmetry.

  (ii) Calculate the angle ϕ to the nearest degree.

  (iii) What fraction of the circumference of the smaller wheel is touching the belt?

  (iv) Calculate the total length of the belt, showing all your working.

M36 (a) Factorise the expression $x^2 - x - 6$.

  (b) Solve the equation $x^2 - x = 6$.

M37 Pauline and Quentin have inherited this plot of land.

(a) Calculate the area of the plot.

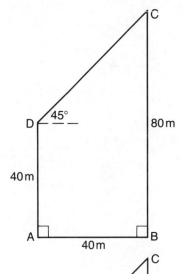

(b) (i) They agree to divide the plot into two equal parts by a straight fence parallel to AD and BC.

Suppose the fence is x metres from AD. Explain why the area to the left of the fence is $40x + \frac{1}{2}x^2$ square metres.

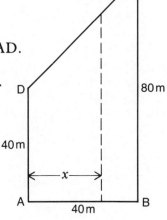

(ii) They want to choose x so as to divide the field as closely as possible into two equal parts. They can measure x to the nearest $0\cdot5$ m. Find by trial and error the value of x they should choose.